Jung

a journey
of transformation

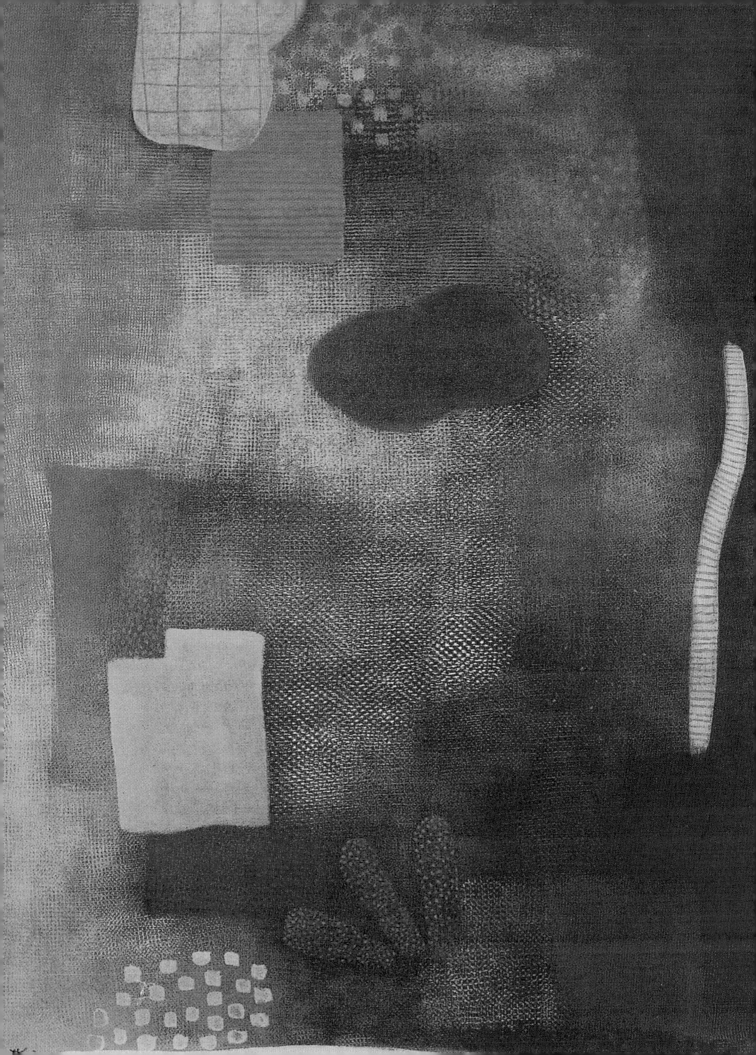

Jung
a journey
of transformation

Exploring his life
and experiencing his ideas

Vivianne Crowley

A publication supported by
THE KERN FOUNDATION

Quest Books
Theosophical Publishing House

Wheaton, Illinois ♦ Chennai (Madras), India

QUEST BOOKS are published by

The Theosophical Society in America,

Wheaton, Illinois 60189–0270,

a branch of a world organization dedicated to the

promotion of the unity of humanity and the

encouragement of the study of religion, philosophy,

and science to the end that we may better understand

ourselves and our place in the universe. The Society stands

for complete freedom of individual search and belief.

For further information about its activities,

write or call 1–800–669–1571, or consult its Web page;

http: //www.theosophical.org

The Theosophical Publishing House

is aided by the generous support of

THE KERN FOUNDATION,

a trust established by Herbert A. Kern

and dedicated to Theosophical education.

Copyright © 1999 Godsfield Press

Text © 1999 Vivianne Crowley

1 2 3 4 5 6 7 8 9 10

First Quest Edition 1999
Copublished with Godsfield Press 1999

For additional information write to
The Theosophical Publishing House
P.O. Box 270
Wheaton, IL 60189-0270
A publication of the Theosophical Publishing House,
a department of the Theosophical Society in America.

Picture research by Vanessa Fletcher
Designed by Sarah Howerd

ISBN 0-8356-0782-8

Library of Congress Cataloging-in-Publication Data

Crowley, Vivianne.
Jung: a journey of transformation / Vivianne Crowley.--1st Quest ed.
    p.   cm.
Includes bibiliographical references and index.
ISBN 0-8356-0782-8
1. Jungian psychology. 2. Psychoanalysis. 3. Jung, C.G. (Carl Gustav),
1875–1961. 4. Self-actualization (Psychology)--Problems, exercises, etc.
I. Title.
BF173.C833   1999
150.19'54'092—dc21   99-31192
[B]   CIP

Printed and bound in Hong Kong

Author's acknowledgments
In grateful thanks for the insights and inspiration provided by Joan and Reyn Swallow, Barbara Somers, and the late Ian Gordon-Brown of the Centre for Transpersonal Psychology, who first taught me Jungian psychology and the exercises in chapters three, eight, and nine of this book.

The publishers wish to thank Intersport and G.F. Sinclair, Ltd.,
both in Lewes, East Sussex, for help with properties.

Special thanks go to Emma Barthes, Terry Burns, Gavin Marle, Rosemary Nobbs, Clive Oxley, Carol Passmore, Christine Post, Julie Robinson, Kevin Scott, Philippa Vaughan, Angela Neal, and Jerry, Hugo, William, and Flora Glenwright for help with photography.

Special thanks to the two contemporary artists featured in this book, Robert Natkin and Freydoon Rassouli, whose work has been influenced by the ideas of Carl Jung. Robert Natkin resides in the U.S.A. and can be contaced by telephone on (203)938-9279, or by fax on (203)938-3791. Rassouli is an Iranian born mystic artist who resides and paints in Southern California. Telephone number (818)995-0726. His artworks can be seen on line at: http://www.Rassouli.com

The painting on page two and five is *Salome* by Robert Natkin.

contents

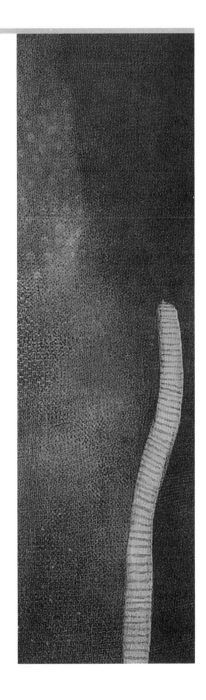

foreword

My encounter with the work of Carl Jung began before I went to university. As a young student I discovered Jung's fascinating book Modern Man in Search of a Soul[1]. I read the book from cover to cover, but understood only a tenth of it. However, it planted a seed. A few months later, I had a sudden realization. I wanted to become a psychologist. I studied psychology at the University of London as an undergraduate and postgraduate and then began a Jungian-oriented training at the Centre for Transpersonal Psychology.

The work of Jung continues to inspire me and forms part of a series of workshops that my husband and I run. I also lecture on the psychology of religion at London University's King's College. This enables me to bring Jung into the undergraduate curriculum.

For me, Jung's work has been an unending source of inspiration, as it has been for so many therapists, doctors, mystics, writers, artists, social scientists, and people in all walks of life. Jung was a man who helped others find their own vision of how to live their lives and of how to find their lives' work. I hope this book will give a flavor of Jung's work and will help you find your own vision, too. Jung looked to the new eon as a time to come of human development, insight, and spiritual evolution. Let us allow his words, ideas, and inspiration to guide us into the new millennium.

Vivianne Crowley

Vivianne Crowley

Summer 1999

---

[1] Carl G. Jung, *Modern Man in Search of a Soul* (1911; reprint, London: Routledge & Kegan Paul, 1973).

Theophanic Light by Rassouli. An understanding of the power of spiritual experience was central to Jung's work.

introduction

Carl Jung is one of the most famous psychologists of our time.

He was born in Switzerland in 1875 and died in 1961.

His life began in the era of the horse-drawn carriage and ended in that of

space travel.

Carl Gustav Jung began his career conventionally enough. He trained first as a doctor and went on to train as a psychiatrist. His life changed radically when he met famous psychiatrist Sigmund Freud. Like Freud, Jung became a major pioneer in the treatment of mental illness through psychotherapy. Ultimately, though, they had professional differences. Freud's interest was primarily in helping people come to terms with childhood traumas in order to adjust to everyday life. Jung wanted to help those with illness and problems; but he also wished to help people whose lives might seem superficial to become more meaningful and creative.

C. G. Jung is world famous as a doctor of the soul. His *Collected Works* fill eighteen volumes and span half a century of writing on psychiatry, psychology, religion, modern politics, ancient myth, and forgotten traditions such as alchemy. Some of his writing is erudite and obscure, but some can be understood easily by anyone. All of it is fascinating. Like many Swiss, Carl Jung switched between the German, English, and French languages with ease. He read Latin and Greek, and conversed with quantum physicists.

Jung loved to travel. He often visited the U.S. where the people were quick to recognize the value of his work — many subsequently traveled to Zürich to train with him. Jung enjoyed speaking English and was a frequent visitor to Britain, where he was warmly greeted. He found the individualism in the U.S. and Britain a welcome contrast to Swiss conformity, and he learned much about European culture and myth.

Jung was also a captain in the Swiss army in World War I. Switzerland has an unusual army, in which every adult Swiss male must serve until retirement, and men spend some weeks each year on military exercises. Jung was quite accustomed to camping, hiking in mountainous regions in tough conditions, and living in conditions of hardship.

Carl Jung working intensely on new ideas and theories in his library.

jung's approach

Jung's love of travel stemmed from a desire to understand people from cultures very different from his own, and he was inspired by Native American, African, Arab, Indian, Tibetan, and Chinese culture. This gave him insight into the common humanity that connects us all and transcends the differences of race, culture, and creed. Jung abhorred colonialism. His meetings with Native Americans and his travels in Africa gave him respect for other traditions, and greater understanding of other cultures. His travels also showed him that his psychological discoveries were part of an ancient wisdom known to sages.

From his study of himself, his patients, and many spiritual traditions, Jung found that the personality we acquire through our upbringing and our social conditioning is only part of what makes us what and who we are. Within us is a deeper and wiser being — the eternal Self, a unique center, a center of consciousness and an archetype of order. This is who we become when all the complex aspects of our personality integrate.

By connecting with the Self, we become individual and different from everyone else, but when we are truly ourselves, we can relate to others in more authentic and meaningful ways. This transformation is difficult, but deep within our psyches at the level of collective unconsciousness is a "map." This is provided by the archetypal images, or "way stations" and "signposts" that lead us on an inner journey of evolution. Each person's journey is different, but Jung showed that there are common patterns of growth.

Jung is surrounded here by alchemical symbols. It was during the second half of his life that exploring alchemy became an important part of his work.

The journey of self-realization is at the heart of the spiritual traditions of all religions. It is a journey to meet the Self and, at the same time, a journey to meet the Divine. Jung believed spiritual experience to be essential to our well-being. He explored the Judeo-Christian tradition of his early life, Catholicism, Hinduism, Buddhism, alchemy, Gnosticism, Zen, and Taoism. His study of world religions showed that each has value, although none is perfect.

Jung did not believe his was the only valid approach to psychology and psychotherapy. This was because he did not believe he necessarily knew all the answers. Jung was a man on an unending journey of discovery that goes beyond the boundaries of a single lifetime.

jung's influence on the world

Jung named his psychotherapy "Analytical Psychology" in order to distinguish it from Freud's own psychoanalysis, and it has become a source of inspiration around the world. The training institutes set up in his name flourish, and his work has been translated into many languages. Ideas drawn from Jungian psychology – Extroversion, Intro-version, Anima, Animus, Self, and Shadow – have entered into our everyday speech and have influenced writers, artists, and filmakers. They have stimulated spiritual seekers within the great world religions, as well as those who walk an individual, un-mapped path.

From each of the great traditions, Jung took spiritual and psychological truths and wove them into his own psychological teachings, all the while emphasizing that his view is not perfect. He believed in personal responsibility rather than dogma or doctrine. Each one of us must make his or her own decisions about truth, based on experience. Jung's way is challenging; it offers no easy answers, but it does offer us the insight and the courage to find our own way. Although he is rooted in the wisdom of the past, Jung is a very modern visionary.

Jung believed that there were two types of people— "introvert" and "extrovert." This man, for example, is an introvert.

the journey

This book introduces the work of Jung to a wider audience. Born in the nine-teenth century and living in the twentieth, Jung was a man whose vision of human evolution and destiny reached into the twenty-first century. He studied the past in order to create a vision for the future.

Jung: A Journey of Transformation explores Jung's life, his major theories, and their rele-vance and impact on our lives today. It explains personality type, Extroversion and Introversion, the masculine and feminine within, Ego and Shadow, as well as the true Self. It describes the journey of self-realization which Jung called "individuation." This is the spir-itual goal of us all.

This book not only helps us to understand ourselves now, but shows us how Jung's insights about the collective unconscious, myth, archetypes, synchronicity, alchemy, Goddess, and the Hero's Quest can help us to transform ourselves. Each chapter contains practical exercises drawn from Jungian and other spiritually-oriented psychologies to explore who we are today and what we can become. We explore our inner psyche to learn how we can evolve in love and wisdom to become who we truly are – and to find the wise person within.

This woman is a typical example of what Jung came to term an "extrovert." Fun-loving and outgoing, she enjoys social events immensely.

jung's childhood

On July 26, 1875, in Switzerland, Emilie Preiswerk Jung, a minister's daughter and the
young wife of the Reverend Paul Achilles Jung, gave birth to her first child, a son.
His parents named him after his grandfather, Carl Gustav Jung,
a medical doctor and university professor.

Jung spent his early childhood in the village of Laufen, which is situated near Switzerland's borders with France and Germany. The Jungs were a poor but well-established family. On the surface all seemed ordinary, but Carl's mother's family, the Preiswerks, were mediums and clairvoyants. It is said that every week, Carl's grandfather, the Reverend Samuel Preiswerk, placed a chair in his study for the ghost of his first wife, who came and talked to him. It is also said that as a child, Carl's mother had to stand behind her father to prevent the spirits from reading over his shoulder when he wrote his sermons.

Jung's mother grew up with an easy acceptance of the paranormal and seems herself to have been something of a clairvoyant. Young Carl was often startled by her mystic utterances. His mother was a good-natured and earthy woman with a zest for life. An extrovert, she liked nothing better than to talk.

In contrast, his father, Paul, was an introvert who loved books and quiet study. He would have preferred a university career to the care of a country parish. Paul Jung's own father was an upstanding citizen of Basel who became Rector of the university and Grand Master of the Swiss Freemasons, but with thirteen children to support, there was little money to go around. Paul Jung, of necessity, had to earn his living and not become a professor.

Jung's parents seemed well matched. As a minister's daughter with six ministers for brothers, Emilie was familiar with the demands of being a minister's wife; but all was not well. Late nineteenth-century families were usually large. Contraception was frowned upon, especially for clergymen, who were expected to fill their homes with a new generation of devout Christians. The Jungs had only two children – Carl and his sister, Gertrud, who was born nine years later. Often Emilie and Paul slept in separate rooms. From time to time, his mother disappeared into hospital with mysterious and unnamed illnesses, but it appears that she might have suffered from depression.

The Pearl by Rassouli. As he was growing up, Jung was surrounded by mediums and
clairvoyants, as well as followers of Christian spirituality.

childhood
and christianity

Carl spent much of the time at home playing alone, particularly before his sister was born, and as a result was an imaginative child. His parents' tensions and mother's illnesses distressed him; at one stage, he developed psychosomatic eczema.

Home could be a depressing place for Carl. The house was near the cemetery where his father conducted funeral services. The open graves, coffins, and attendants in their black coats were frightening

for a young boy. Sometimes drowned suicide and accident victims were dragged from the river nearby. One body was even laid out in the Jungs' garden shed. Carl was told that "Lord Jesus" takes dead souls to himself, but the young boy didn't understand what this meant. He became suspicious of Jesus, this supposedly loving figure, who caused people to disappear and be buried in muddy graves.

As the child of a Protestant minister, Carl Jung was surrounded by religion. His father's study was full of theology books, and at family gatherings there could be seven or more clergymen around the table. It seems, though, that Paul Jung was unhappy in his vocation. He studied and preached Christianity, but appears himself never to have had a deep spiritual experience. Theoretically, he knew all about God; the problem was he seemed never to have met him. Carl was acutely aware of his father's doubts and crises of faith.

Carl did not like going to church. He loved Christmas and the Christmas tree, but the lengthy sermons during the rest of the year left him unmoved. He hoped that all would be different when he could finally receive communion. This first happens in the Protestant Swiss Reformed Church at confirmation. Carl looked forward in anticipation to the moment when he would receive the body of Christ into himself at confirmation. It seemed to him to be a profound spiritual mystery.

Churches were a major part of Jung's early life, although he did not ever really enjoy attending services.

Jung found Christianity hard to reconcile with his own spiritual experiences but loved Christmas celebrations.

Carl prepared for his own confirmation with great seriousness and went expecting much. He stood in his new dark suit with the men of the congregation to drink the thin sour wine and to eat the flat bread. Impatiently, he waited for the mystical revelation, the divine rapture, the sense of the presence of God within himself. But nothing happened at all. He looked at the men at his side. Nothing appeared to be happening for them either. To the idealistic young teenager, it seemed there was no spiritual experience to be had there. The ceremony seemed like a travesty – an absence rather than a presence of God – and he was determined never to participate in it again.

growing up fast

Carl had some reservations about orthodox Christianity, but despite them, he became a deeply spiritual teenager who felt drawn to pray to God. Like many only children who spend a lot of time with adults, he matured quickly. He was highly intelligent and full of questions like, "Why did God create Adam and Eve so they could sin?" "Why does evil exist?" "What does the Trinity really mean?" His school friends called him "Father Abraham." Paul Jung felt unable to deal with his son's questioning since he, himself, was not sure of the answers. His only answer was to tell his son to stop thinking and simply believe.

The young Carl Jung. This picture was taken in 1881, when he was six years old.

education

arl passed his examinations, but his school years bored him. Few of his teachers appreciated his endless questions, and many even dismissed him as stupid. He was highly indignant when he handed in an essay that was so good his teacher immediately accused him of copying it from elsewhere.

Choosing a career was not an easy task for Carl. Thanks to his father's library and his own curiosity, Carl was widely read. The problem was that he was interested in everything. Switzerland is unusual because it has three major languages, and Carl enjoyed learning them; he was born in the German-speaking region, but quickly became fluent in French and, later, English. He also learned Latin and Greek. He loved philosophy and read Kant, Goethe, Hartmann, Schopenhauer, and Nietzsche. Science also fascinated him. Archaeology and the mysteries of the past were another lifelong interest; but there was no archaeology faculty at Basel and too little money to send him away to study. Theology interested him, but his unorthodox ideas made the ministry impossible. What was he to do?

Guided by his dreams, Carl decided to allow his love of

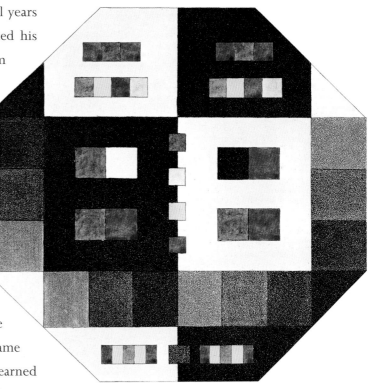

This plate shows Goethe's "Theory of Colour." Carl was deeply impressed by reading Goethe's work. It was rumored that he was descended from Goethe.

science to take him into his paternal grandfather's profession – he would study medicine. In spring 1895, at the age of nineteen, Carl began his medical studies at Basel University. He loved his new-found freedom. Like a typical introvert, Carl did better in education the farther he went and the freer he was to pursue his own interests.

At school, Carl had many friends but few whose minds were as lively and curious as his own was. An introverted minister's son with interests beyond his years, Carl might have found himself bullied if he had not had the good fortune to grow to over six feet and

The work of Friedrich Nietzsche was of great interest to Carl, and he was an avid reader of the philosopher throughout his adolescent years.

be built like a lumberjack. However, at university he felt much more at ease. He found likeminded friends and could express the extroverted side of his nature more easily. He joined his father's old fraternity and became socially confident. He made a new circle of fun-loving and extroverted friends who liked nothing better than to join in philosophical debates over brimming tankards of beer. He learned to work hard and play hard. He became a leading light in the student drinking club, sometimes staying up all night in the bar drinking and talking. He could drink so much beer his friends called him "the barrel."

Carl enjoyed debating immensely and eventually became a charismatic speaker. His leadership potential began to show through, and his professors warmed to the enthusiastic and questioning student in a way his teachers at school had not. They began to think of posts for him after graduation. The way was being paved for Carl – a glittering medical career, full of possibility, was opening up for him.

Carl (middle row, center) as a student in Basel in 1896. He is seen here surrounded by the university friends with whom he used to enjoy drinking and debating.

"Although we must say of the transcendental concepts of reason that they are only ideas, this is not by any means to be taken as signifying that they are superfluous and void. For even if they cannot determine any object, they may yet, in a fundamental and unobserved fashion, be of service to the understanding as a canon for its extended and consistent employment."[1]

[1] Immanuel Kant, *Immanuel Kant's Critique of Pure Reason* (London and New York: Norman Kemp Smith, 1929), 319ff

personality orientations

two personality attitudes

From an early age, Carl Jung was aware of two personality orientations. His mother was outgoing and interested in the world around her while his father was withdrawn and interested in the inner world. He was also aware of these different tendencies within himself. Later, he named them "extroversion" and "introversion."

extroversion

Extroverts understand the world around them and respond accordingly. As children, they are physically well coordinated, and they learn early how to play games. They are not afraid of rough and tumble play, but are also happy to be huggy, touchy, and feely. Extroverts do not need much personal space, and they find it easy to share their toys or a multibunk dormitory at summer camp. They love parties and are quickly bored if there is no one to play with. Extroverted children are sociable and make friends quickly.

sociability

At college, extroverts join clubs, fraternities, and sororities. They volunteer as organizers and become social movers. They lend people their cars, their clothes, their money. They talk about their latest loves. They love noise, bustle, and buzz. They want to communicate — they strike up conversations while standing in line at the supermarket checkout, in the airport departure lounge, in the pizza parlor. When extroverts start work, they can share an apartment

Extroverted people particularly enjoy socializing at parties.

with five other people. This is paradise for them because there is usually someone at home to talk to. Extroverts need an audience and someone to listen to them. They find out what they think by talking their ideas through with others rather than thinking them through in their heads. Extroverts love brainstorming meetings, discussions, arguments, and debates.

jobs

Extroverts can be too busy juggling their social, sporting, academic, and part-time job interests to graduate with absolutely top grades – but they are still snapped up in the job market. They network and find contacts. They know how to be interviewed and make the right impression. Extroverts do well in large companies. They remember people's names and know how to work the system. Since extroverts enjoy companionship any situation where they can lead a group or manage a team gives them just the stimulation they need. Extroverts can make charismatic leaders.

Extroverts have good presentation skills. They like meeting new people, communicating, and traveling. They make excellent sales people, marketing managers, bartenders, retail managers, public relations workers, politicians, and fashion, media, and advertising executives. They understand the public pulse and know what people want to hear. Extroverts love demanding jobs that have an element of

The hustle and bustle of a busy stock exchange is the perfect environment for an extrovert.

time pressure, competitiveness, adventure, and/or danger. The armed forces, firefighters, lifeguards, gym teachers, safari leaders, mountain expedition leaders, and medical emergency teams are all jobs that appeal to the more physical extrovert.

An athletic extrovert can meet the physical and social challenges involved in being a gym teacher.

personality orientations

introversion

Introverted children have good concentration. They are likely to enjoy reading and studying, and may be ahead of their age group when they start school. It is important, though, that introverted children have time to adjust to being in large groups. They may enjoy attending school more if they have been to kindergarten first, so they have readymade friends when they go to school.

Introverts enjoy solitary activities such as reading, which also makes use of their high level of concentration.

Introverted children enjoy being alone but need to be encouraged to play with friends.

notice me

Introverts are thought of as shy, but there are shy extroverts as well as shy introverts. Introverts enjoy making an impact, but only when they are in control of the situation. Many performers are extroverts but there is a substantial proportion who are introverts. As actors, musicians, singers or dancers, introverts can enjoy the applause of the crowd by being someone else. They can display great emotions, but never let the public see their own. "I want to be alone," actress and introvert Greta Garbo said famously. A press conference in front of pushy reporters would not be an introvert's favorite scenario.

friendship

The stereotypical introvert is someone who hates parties but, like all generalizations, this is not always true. Introverts often do like parties – providing they know most of the guests. A room full of strangers is an off-putting sight for an introvert, so they are selective about the parties they attend. They do not leap into new relationships, but prefer to get to know people slowly. They would rather have a small circle of trusted, reliable, and longterm friends than a crowd of acquaintances. An introverted friend is a friend for life. Introverts make considerable efforts to keep in touch with friends, even at long distance. E-mail is a wonderful invention for introverts.

commitment

Introverts have slower physiological reactions than extroverts. A plus side is that they are less impulsive and are less likely to have accidents. Introverts are cautious and like to weigh up the options before making a decision. Faced with a sudden decision, introverts are more likely to say "No" than "Yes," but they are more reliable than extroverts. Once introverts make a decision or take on a commitment, they are likely to stick with it. Introverts need personal space and are good at doing things alone. They have the patience to learn complex skills and to perfect them. They also have the patience and dedication to undergo long programs of solitary training. Field and track, competitive swimming, or tennis are more likely to appeal than team sports like football.

at work

Introverts have the patience needed for long study to gain professional qualifications. Doctors, lawyers, judges, accountants, engineers, librarians, computer specialists, and mechanics are more likely to be introverts. Introverts like to be good at doing a few well-chosen jobs or activities instead of trying to cram in as many different experiences as possible. They are more likely to become leaders when they are older, and employers realize the value of their expertise. Introverts think deeply and may arrive at truly original and creative ideas in art, technology, or science. Great leaps forward in scientific thinking or the creation of a new form of novel are more likely to come from introverts.

Introverted athletes can excel in individual competitive sports. They have the dedication and motivation to undergo long hours of solitary training.

no absolutes

a matter of physiology

No one is completely introverted or extroverted. Introverts can become quite extroverted in situations that are familiar to them and where they feel comfortable and can be relaxed. Extroverts can become introverted when they are particularly depressed. However, our basic orientation, and how we react to the outside world, is physiologically determined.

The extrovert leaps in where angels fear to tread. The introvert steps back from danger, thinks about it, and then goes on the attack when they feel they are prepared. Extroverts are easily distracted from what they are doing, while introverts usually have much longer attention spans.

Extroversion and introversion are not the result of our upbringing — we can find extroverts and introverts within the same family. Even small babies will display the differences in their attitudes to the world. But there are also what Jung calls "abnormal" situations — where parents are so extremely extroverted or introverted that they force their children to conform to their own orientation. If this happens to us, we are not being true to ourselves and have become what someone else wants us to be, rather than what we really are. If we have been forced to react in ways that are against our nature for long periods of time then we may become neurotic or ill.

A family unit can be made up of both introverts and extroverts as each person is an individual.

problems of extroversion

Extroverts like to talk, even if they have nothing worthwhile to say. The extreme extrovert is overly loud and never listens to others. Sometimes they would do better to stop talking and trying to entertain their friends. Their friends do not always want to be entertained. Rather, they want their extrovert friend to listen to them. Extroverts can forget conversation is a two-way process. They also tend not to monitor their own reactions; they can be so busy meeting the demands of the busy schedules they have created for themselves that they do not stop and ask themselves whether they are happy with the lifestyle they have created. Extroverts can struggle for a long time with depression before they notice that something is wrong.

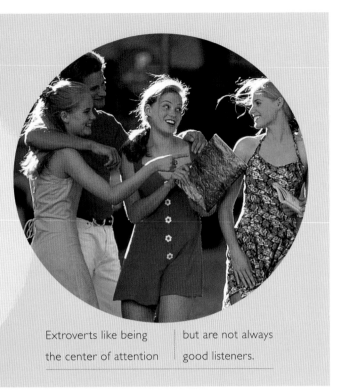

Extroverts like being the center of attention | but are not always good listeners.

Introverts like doing things alone and can become engrossed by projects. Unfortunately this can | have an adverse effect on their friendships, as there is little opportunity to meet new people.

problems of introversion

For the extreme introvert, everyone else has to do all the running, initiate all the contact, and make all the conversation. As children, introverts can be too mature for their years. They are interested in the world of ideas, imagination, and spirituality. Other children may find them odd. Life transitions, such as college to work, or moving home and job, can be difficult. It means meeting a completely new set of people with new expectations. Introverts may lack the confidence to push themselves and their ideas. They may undersell themselves and settle for jobs or relationships that are below their potential. Introverts worry about telephoning their friends in case they get them at an inconvenient moment. Would-be friends or partners may interpret their behavior as lack of interest, when really introverts are desperately interested but do not know how to say so.

introvert or extrovert?

Now you have read the descriptions of both introversion and extroversion, you may have guessed what your own orientation is. Remember, if you are an extrovert, you can have crises of self-doubt when you withdraw into your shell, but they will be short-lived. They do not mean you are an introvert.

You may be an introvert, but you may also have learned to disguise it. In social situations with people you know, you may be the life and soul of the party, so people may mistake you for an extrovert. It is only when you leave the party, with a sigh of relief you can now switch off, that you let your introversion show.

If you are not sure where your orientation lies, here are some statements to help you. See which list, introversion or extroversion, produces the most "yes" responses for you.

An extrovert should try calming meditation, while an introvert may need to pick up a phone rather than wait for it to ring.

introversion

		yes	no
1	You would rather have your own apartment than share with lots of people.		
2	You prefer parties where you know most of the guests.		
3	You enjoy spending a quiet evening alone.		
4	You prefer to plan ahead rather than to deal constantly with the unexpected.		
5	You are modest about telling people your achievements.		
6	People telephone you more than you telephone them.		
7	You find it difficult to remember people's names.		
8	You enjoy talking to people but find it tiring.		
9	You are a good listener.		
10	You find it easier to learn from books rather than being shown.		
11	You prefer one-to-one discussions rather than addressing large groups.		
12	You like having visitors, but are often relieved when they go home.		
13	You are good at keeping secrets.		
14	In a new group you prefer to let others take the lead.		

extroversion

		yes	no
1	People often choose you to run teams or organize events.		
2	You like organizing events and making sure people have a good time.		
3	You are full of ideas and projects for your friends and colleagues to carry out.		
4	You like networking.		
5	You are easily bored if you find yourself alone.		
6	People sometimes think you tactless.		
7	You like group vacations.		
8	You frequently interrupt people and finish their sentences for them.		
9	You enjoy doing new things.		
10	You prefer newspapers and magazines to books.		
11	You feel stimulated and energized by crowds.		
12	You enjoy busy restaurants and crowded bars.		
13	You hate to eat alone.		
14	You are stimulated by crises and having to think on your feet.		

valuing our opposite: introverts

Although we are predominantly introvert or extrovert, we can learn to balance our introversion or extroversion. There are specific things that an introvert can do:

• Learn to take the initiative – strike up conversations with people who interest you.

• Take a course in public speaking – you might never feel totally at ease giving presentations, but you can enjoy them once you start.

• Learn to say "I'll come back to you" if offered an unexpected opportunity - don't immediately say "No." Go away and think for half an hour. Then give your answer.

• Pick up the phone and arrange a social event – don't wait for people to invite you.

valuing our opposite: extroverts

Extroverts can also take steps to balance themselves: so that their hidden introverted side can surface to balance their personality:

• Learn to listen – if there are five people in a discussion, do not talk more than thirty percent of the time.

• Slow down – it can be fun to make decisions quickly, but have you thought through all the implications?

• Learn to say "No" – if you take on too much, you will not be able to do things properly and on time, and people will then begin to think you unreliable.

• Listen to your inner voice – you can be so busy doing things that you don't notice how you feel. Record your dreams; go on a meditation weekend or a spiritual retreat.

jung discovers a map

As Jung began his university career, his father became ill.
Doctors could not diagnose the cause, but he complained of severe abdominal
pains and gradually became an invalid. At the end of Jung's first year at
university his father died, leaving very little money.

Jung had to take control of the family budget – he could not pay the bills at their large house, so the family moved to a smaller house just outside Basel but near enough to walk to university. One of his uncles gave money to support his mother, and another loaned him money to finish his studies. He got some part-time work and sold antiques for an aunt on commission.

From his childhood on, Jung was interested in the world of the mind. One of his cousins, Hélène Preiswerk, was a medium and held regular séances that Jung attended. He meticulously recorded the phenomena Hélène produced. Jung's early experiences of these séances became the material for his doctoral dissertation.

Paranormal activity also sometimes happened when his mother was present. Carl Jung was at home one day, studying in a room adjoining the dining room where she was sitting, when there was a loud noise like a pistol shot. Their round walnut dining table had split right from one edge to the center. Two weeks later, Jung returned home to find that his mother, sister, and the maid had heard another crack from a nineteenth-century sideboard. A bread knife blade in the sideboard had shattered into several pieces. Jung took the knife to an expert, but no faults in the steel could be found, and the expert had no explanation for what had happened.

Jung was never good at pursuing topics that bored him, and the psychiatry lectures he had attended were uninspiring. When it came to his final examinations, he put off psychiatry revision until the very last. When finally he picked up the psychiatry textbook, it was a revelation. He had a vision of what would be his life's work. When Jung began to read about psychiatry, he discovered a topic that brought together all his interests – medicine, the nature of consciousness, and the paranormal.

Conception by Rassouli. It was when Jung picked up a psychiatry textbook to study for his final medical examinations that he found the seed of what was to become his life's work.

his early career

The Director of the Medical Clinic at Basel University had noticed Jung's talents. When Jung graduated, the director offered him a prestigious post, but Jung turned it down in favor of a career in psychiatry. At that time, psychiatry was one of the most poorly paid sectors of the medical profession.

His professors at the university were aghast. Psychiatry offered little prestige, and the treatments available were limited. Patients were usually locked in psychiatric hospitals until they got well spontaneously or died. His friends thought Jung was insane to want such a career, but he was extremely determined. On December 11, 1900, he became First Assistant Physician at the Burghölzi Clinic just outside Zürich. The Burghölzi was no ordinary psychiatric hospital, but one of the leading establishments of its day. Patients came from many countries to be treated by its head, Dr. Eugen Bleuler, and his team.

Dr. Bleuler was a man of great humanity who was devoted to his patients and endeavored to recruit the best young doctors of his day for his clinic. For Dr. Bleuler, psychiatry was a vocation, and he expected Jung to be completely dedicated. Workers at the clinic were forbidden to drink alcohol – on the premises or off it. This came as something of a shock to Jung after his student drinking days. He had to live at the hospital, and there were no late nights – he had to be in by 10 P.M. Jung found that he worked very long days. He had to talk with his patients every day and write up detailed case notes late into the night. However, although Bleuler was demanding, his training was excellent and standards remained high.

Jung was an original, and his apprenticeship showed him to be that rare being – an innovator who could take the best from others and incorporate it into his own work. In this portrait of him at the age of twenty-eight, determination and humanity can be read in his expression.

Bleuler wanted the Burghölzi to be at the leading edge of psychiatry. There was an active research program, and Jung worked hard at this, writing papers for publication on the word-association technique. He also attended seminars that discussed the new theories and techniques, including those of the Austrian psychiatrist, Sigmund Freud. Jung was impressed by Freud's insights on dream interpretation, and in 1906, he sent Freud some of his research papers.

~The feeling-toned complex...
brings about subjective and
treacherous reactions and arouses
associations the meaning of
which is utterly unexpected by
the ego-complex~ [1]

"Occurrences of everyday life are nothing but association experiments on a major scale."

"...there exists something that cannot be put on paper: namely those imponderables of human contact..which affect only our unconscious."

schizophrenia

Jung's contact with patients helped him to develop new insights, particularly into schizophrenia. Until this time, schizophrenics had been dismissed as "mad." Bleuler taught Jung to listen to his patients over long periods of time. As empathy developed, Jung was able to understand them and discovered patterns and meanings in what, at first, seemed to be random fantasies and ramblings. In these lay clues to the source of each patient's illness and to its cure. One patient, who had been in the hospital for almost forty years, continually moved her hands up and down. Something about the gesture reminded Jung of a cobbler making shoes before mechanization. When he asked the patient's brother what precipitated her illness, he discovered that she had been betrothed to a shoemaker who had jilted her. Ever since, the sad patient had imitated the hand actions of her lost love.

[1] R. Steele, *Freud & Jung: Conflicts of Interpretation* (London: Routledge & Kegan Paul, 1982), 177-178, and 180.

jung and freud

By now, Jung was Bleuler's second-in-command at the clinic, and he also held an academic post in psychiatry at the University of Zürich similar to that of an American assistant professor. Freud was delighted to hear from the talented young Swiss and sensed that Jung might be extremely valuable to the growing psychoanalytic movement.

Freud invited Carl and his wife Emma to visit him in Vienna in 1907. They traveled by train from Zürich to the Austrian capital. The journey took them eastward through mountains and Austria's long valleys to romantic Vienna, famous for many delightful things; musicians like Mozart, coffee shops, pastries, and the waltz. Freud greeted Carl and Emma at their hotel with a bouquet of flowers and invited them to lunch with himself and his family.

The meeting went well, but Jung immediately had some reservations. He and Freud talked about Freud's theories that adult behavior is influenced by early experiences, such as weaning, potty training, and how we are taught to deal with sexual desire. If a person experiences difficulty or trauma at any stage of his or her development – oral, anal, or sexual – the seeds are sown for later neurosis. For Freud, the sexual impulse was the most powerful impulse of all, and he believed that most neuroses related to repressed sexual desires. Jung agreed that sexuality was indeed important, but not to the same extent. He also sensed that, for Freud, his "sexual theory" had become a kind of religious dogma, and this worried Jung intensely. After the meeting, Jung had a dream that he was trapped in the narrow winding streets of a ghetto and could not get out.

Freud's Vienna was a fertile ground for new thoughts and beliefs. In the late nineteenth century it had been famous for its culture; by the 1900s it housed one of the most forward-looking scientific communities.

Dear Professor Freud,
...it seems to me that though the genesis of hysteria is predominantly, it is not exclusively, sexual. I take exactly the same view of your sexual theory.
With many thanks,
Very truly yours,
C.G. Jung

Dear Colleague,
Your writings have long led me to suspect that your appreciation of my psychology does not extend to all my views on hysteria and the problem of sexuality. But I venture to hope that in the course of the years you will come much closer to me than you now think possible.
Yours very sincerely
Dr. Freud.[1]

[1] William McGuire, ed., *The Freud/Jung Letters* (Princeton: Princeton University Press, 1974), 4–5.

father and son
master and pupil?

"We met at one o'clock and talked virtually non-stop for 13 hours. Freud was the first man of real importance I had encountered; in my experience up to then no one else could compare with him. There was nothing the least trivial in his attitude. I found him extremely intelligent, shrewd, and altogether remarkable. And yet my first impressions of him remain somewhat tangled; I could not make him out." [1]

Whatever the difficulties that arose between them later, the first meeting Jung had with Freud was highly significant. It was to set Jung's life on its course toward developing his own school of psychotherapy. A strong relationship developed between the two men; Jung was nineteen years younger than Freud, fatherless, and a newcomer in Freud's field of psychiatry. The two men's emotional needs, their discrepancy in age, and similarity in interests made it easy for a father-and-son relationship to evolve. Freud had many followers in Vienna, but none of Jung's intellectual caliber. Jung's well-informed mind provided Freud with badly needed intellectual stimulation. Jung, for his part, considered Freud the most remarkable person he had met in his life. He became an enthusiastic advocate for Sigmund Freud's form of psychotherapy – psychoanalysis. Freud and Jung's first meeting led to a prolific exchange of letters, and further meetings followed.

The two men had similar interests. Both trained as medical doctors but were fascinated by a poorly paid, unpopular branch of medicine. Both were innovative thinkers who were to make their mark on the twentieth century. Both were also strong-minded individualists who were incapable of being followers of anyone else. As such, they were doomed to clash. Freud was looking for disciples, not collaborators; Jung admired Freud but he was not looking for a guide.

Freud (bottom left), and Jung (bottom right), together with other medical colleagues in September 1909 at Clark University, Worcester, Massachusetts.

[1] C. G. Jung, *Memories, Dreams, Reflections* (New York: Viking Penguin, 1982), 23.

important jungian concepts

the hidden psyche

Freud and Jung both believed that the mind, or psyche, has two levels. The conscious mind is the part of ourselves that we know. There is also a deeper level, which contains all the thoughts, feelings, images, and sensory impressions that we have repressed, suppressed, or may simply not have noticed.

Freud named this level the subconscious. This deeper level contains biological urges such as aggression and sexuality, which society teaches us to control and repress. Our repressed thoughts, feelings, and memories

Freud had many ideas about the psyche that Jung shared, although Jung did not agree with all his theories.

are "forgotten." Normally we cannot easily recall them, but they can appear spontaneously in dream and fantasy, whenever the conscious mind's grip on the psyche slackens.

When we suppress feelings or ideas, we thrust them out of consciousness so we can concentrate on something else. We might have a fight with our partner before we leave home for work. During the day, we might have to ignore our anger in order to deal with new, unrelated situations, but as soon as we return home, we can easily let that anger surface again. Unlike repression, all our suppressed thoughts, feelings, and memories are freely accessible to us.

We also have subliminal perceptions — thoughts, feelings, and impressions that are too fleeting or weak to register in our consciousness. They can give us information about events, aspects of someone's personality, or implications of a situation that we did not consciously notice at the time. Hypnosis of witnesses to crime works on this principle.

The world of the psyche is full of images and impressions that have an unconscious effect on our lives.

archetypes

The collective unconscious is the term Jung used for the psychic contents that are not just common to an individual but are open to us all. This unconscious is our inheritance and is the home of the archetypes, a word derived from Greek *arch*, meaning origin, and *tupos*, meaning imprint. The archetypes are forces that cause inner transformation. They are symbols and energy patterns that appear universally, in all cultures, historical periods, and geographical locations. Jung believed that through the archetypes we have a tendency to reproduce similar mythical ideas in all cultures and at all periods of history. If through some global disaster civilization is destroyed, the archetypes will provide an inner patterning that will allow us to regenerate our culture and spirituality from the ashes of the past. Some archetypal images that appear in myth include the Great Mother Goddess, the Wise Old Man, the Magician, and the Sun Child of magical birth who represents the forces of good and must struggle with his evil dark twin for control of the world. The archetypal images are so powerful that if they arise in our dreams and visions they enthrall us. They have what Jung called a "numinous" quality. They are fascinating, for good or ill.

a personal and collective unconscious

Jung accepted Freud's ideas about the hidden psyche, but believed it did not just contain material from the past. He believed it was also the source of new ideas and creative inspirations that would emerge into conscious awareness in the future. He called this the personal unconscious.

If we were in touch with the unconscious, we would be in touch with our creative source. We would also be in contact with an even deeper level of the human psyche. Jung called this the collective unconscious, a storehouse of inherited instincts and universal archetypal ideas of humankind that have evolved over millennia of human existence and are the origin of symbol and myth.

Jung continued to develop his ideas on the conscious and unconscious levels of our beings throughout his career.

jung's aim
and methods

the journey

People are drawn to Jungian analysis for many different reasons. For some, the aim is to cure problems that are causing distress and impeding their progress in life and that is where it ends. For others, the goal is to go beyond "healed normality" to reach the stage of self-realization or individuation. Jung treated each person as an individual and varied his methods accordingly, but his therapy does have four distinct stages.

confession

The first stage is confession. This involves personal revelation – telling the therapist about things that we hide from others; such as our guilts, inadequacies, and fears. This is never easy, but it is extremely important to trust the therapist.

The Jungian analyst must also help us uncover things that we are unaware of hiding. Revealing these hidden experiences can bring about catharsis, a cleansing that releases repressed emotion. When we no longer have anything to hide, we can experience an enormous sense of release from the heavy burden of concealment.

Working with an analyst enables us to understand our emotions and reactions. An analyst can help us reach an explanation for our problems and will work gently through this sometimes painful process.

Confessing things we have kept hidden from everyone else is not easy, but the analyst will listen with understanding as you unburden yourself, in order to help you access your repressed emotions.

elucidation

The second stage of the process, elucidation, is referred to by some Jungians as "explanation." Explanations are found as to what are the sources of our problems and these bring understanding. As the relationship with the analyst deepens, a transference can occur. We are novices in a new territory, the analyst is the expert. There is an element of teacher and pupil, parent and child, in the relationship. We may transfer to the analyst any feelings, issues, and problems that we experienced with authority figures in the past.

education

Education is the third stage. Knowing about the problems of the past may not be enough to give us solutions for the future. We need to know how to move forward to enable us to change future behavior. This stage of the process aims to get us functioning, so we can live our everyday lives and fulfill our responsibilities as adults in society. For many, this will be the ultimate aim of a Jungian analysis.

Untitled painting by Robert Natkin. Opening the door to our unconscious to learn how to deal with our future and the pain of the past is the aim of Jungian analysis.

transformation

There may be some of us that come to Jungian analysis with lives that are already satisfactory by all the standard measures of society. We have a good job, well-adjusted children, a faithful partner whom we love. We have it all; but still there is something missing. We feel stuck or imprisoned. This is a theme often found in myth and fairytale. We are like Ali Baba confronted with a door that we do not know how to open. We sense only that on the other side there is a treasure that is beyond price. We seek the magic word that will open the door. Jungian analysis can help us to go deep within ourselves to open the gates to the unconscious. Here we can find new insights to enable us to move forward. Jung named this part of analysis "transformation," and it is this final stage that leads to individuation, greater maturity, and individuality.

the purpose of life

As he came to understand the deeper level of the human psyche, Jung then began to evolve a vision about the purpose of life. We are born, perhaps reproduce, and die. Was this a meaningless wheel of death and life, or was there something more? Jung believed there was much more.

individuation

Jung saw individuation as the most important goal in life – the process by which we become truly ourselves. We evolve and eventually arrive at true self-acceptance and integration. It is a challenge to us all, a spiritual adventure and our own personal Grail Quest. It means that all masks and pretense must be stripped away. In the process of individuation, we each find our own true vocation – our life's work and what it is we are meant to do. For each of us has a unique destiny and a significant role to play in the great human drama.

archetypal encounters

As we begin to open ourselves to the unconscious, we become aware of the archetypes of the Shadow, our inferior side; the Anima or Animus, our contra-sexual side; and, finally, the true Self. The Self can appear in dreams and visions in the guise of a Wise Old Man or Woman, or the Sun Child. It can also appear as more abstract symbols such as the Sun itself, a mandala, a flower of great purity, or a rare and precious jewel or treasure. The role of the analyst or therapist is to help us understand and access the unconscious archetypes that influence our journey.

Dreams often capture our unconscious reactions to everyday situations.

Recognizing this can help us to learn what messages our dreams hold for us.

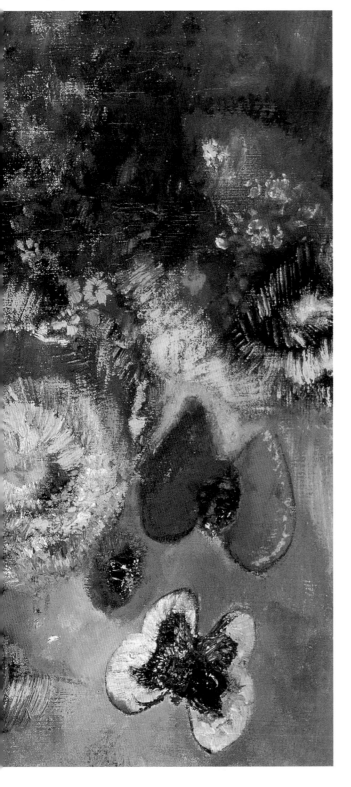

dreamwork

Jungian analysis depends on our accessing material from the unconscious. But how are we to access it? One gateway is through our dreams. Each night our brains process the events of the day, storing them in memory. Dream material contains more than just our conscious awareness of events. Our brains can only focus on so many things at once, and we are aware of only a limited part of what happens to us each day. We may, for example, meet someone, but our minds are focused on our next appointment. We do not really register what the individual is saying, or how she is saying it. Later we dream we are standing by a tree whose branches suddenly encircle and trap us. We struggle to get free and notice that the tree has a face, the face of the woman we met earlier that day. We are startled and wake up. What might such a dream tell us?

With a dream such as the one described, we could employ another technique – active imagination. We might imagine the dream scene just described and ask the face in the tree why she is doing this to us. Why is she trying to trap us? Is she jealous – or simply afraid of us? Does the person feel threatened by us in some way? How can we help her feel less threatened? By entering into an interior dialogue with the components of our dreams, we can find out what messages they have for us. We can also use this technique to analyze the archetypes that arise in our fantasies and creative work.

Each one of us dreams, but very few of us try to understand our dreams.

dreams and dreaming

Dreams offer us important information that can help us in everyday life. Some people protest that they never remember dreams; but once you have broken through into your dream life, you will find you can recall them easily. Your brain will get into the habit, once it knows what you require.

Make it a habit to write down the contents of your dreams as soon as you wake up: otherwise you will find it difficult to recall the vital details.

recording your dreams

To learn to recall our dreams, it is important to record them immediately. Keep a pen and paper, computer, or cassette recorder beside your bed. As soon as you wake up, record your dreams immediately and before you talk to anyone. If you leave it for even a minute, you will have lost much of the important detail. If you still cannot remember anything, and if you have a tolerant partner, try waking yourself every two or three hours for a few nights. You will then wake up right in the middle of your dreams, and it will be much easier to record them.

dream themes

To analyze your dreams, look for recurring patterns and themes. If you find that you persistently dream about someone you love in a negative way, it does not mean that the relationship is 90 percent negative. It does mean that there are hidden tensions and issues that need to be explored. An example of hidden tension is in a recurrent dream that one man had. He was traveling home on his usual train and, instead of getting off at his home station, he would carry on to the airport, catch a plane, and fly away. It took him a long time to realize that he was unhappy in his job, and this dream was showing that he longed to "fly away." The recurring dreams stopped when he left the job and tried the career he had always wanted.

unpacking our dreams

When analyzing your dreams, think first whether their meaning is literal. If you dream that your car breaks down, it may be that you subliminally heard a strange engine noise. So does your car need checking? If the answer is no, then think about what a vehicle might represent for you. Think about where the car was going when it broke down. Was it to work? To see a lover? How did you feel about not reaching your destination – disappointment, anger, relief? Note your feelings in the dream. Was there any occasion the previous day when you had the same feelings? What was this occasion? Who was there? Might the dream relate to that incident? Remember, most dreams are triggered by incidents the day before.

dialogue

To obtain more information, you could use active imagination and enter into dialogue with different aspects of your dream. Ask the car why it has broken down. One lady had a recurrent dream that a small, lively mouse was living in the basement of her house, but she couldn't understand what it meant. So she sat in a quiet room and imagined the dream scenario. Then she asked the mouse if it would explain what it was doing. It answered "I may be a mouse, but I'm a pretty big and powerful mouse. And I get things done." She realized that the mouse represented her. The images that appear in our dreams often have messages for us and want to help us.

Winchester by Robert Natkin. Images and symbols in your dreams, however abstract, may have particular significance for you.

Sitting alone quietly and mentally re-entering a dream can help you find its meaning.

persona and ego

Carl Jung first visited the United States in 1909 at the invitation of Professor G. Stanley Hall, the founding editor of the American Journal of Psychology. Jung and Freud were to be guest speakers at a conference to celebrate the twentieth anniversary of the founding of Clark University, Worcester, Massachusetts.

This was before the age of the airplane; Freud and Jung sailed to New York by oceanliner. The liner hit fog and steamed forward like a ghostly monster. Only the dark waves immediately around the ship were visible. The fog deadened all sound except the eerie foghorns. To pass the time, the psychiatrists analyzed one another's dreams. This seems foolish, given the mistrust that was building up between them; before embarkation, Freud had a fainting fit in their hotel and accused Jung of harboring a death wish toward him. Jung believed that some of Freud's dreams revealed adulterous longings toward his sister-in-law. Not surprisingly, Freud was unwilling to discuss this. The dream analysis ceased.

Freud and Jung's lectures drew large crowds, despite the language barrier of lecturing in German, and they were widely reported in the press. At the conference, they both received honorary doctorates, one of the highest academic honors. This marked an important acceptance of psychoanalytic theory.

Jung had worried that Americans would be much too puritanical to accept Freud's ideas about sexuality. Instead, he found open-minded people who were eager for new learning. Jung noticed many contrasts between the United States and his homeland. Switzerland was full of rules and regulations. On public signs written in German, everything was "verboten" or forbidden. In the U.S., notices made polite requests.

In New York, there was time for sightseeing. They visited Chinatown, Coney Island, the Metropolitan Museum of Art, and Tiffany's. In a Manhattan cinema, they saw their first movie. The famous Harvard professor, James Jackson Putnam, invited them to his family's summer camp in the Adirondack Mountains near Lake Placid. Jung scaled the 6,000-foot mountain peaks to gaze in wonder over virgin forest. The scale of the countryside was a complete contrast to tiny Switzerland. Jung fell in love with it, and it was to be the first of many such trips across the Atlantic.

Voyager by Rassouli. It was during their first trip to the United States that the tension between Freud and Jung began to reach unbearable levels.

old bull
young lion

Tensions and rivalries were developing between Freud the Taurus and Jung the Leo. These were becoming obvious to Freud's followers if not to Freud himself. On their return from the United States, Freud insisted on making Jung the Permanent President of the International Psychoanalytic Society. He was marking out the younger man as his successor as leader of the psychoanalytic movement.

Why was Jung so important to Freud? Freud was impressed by Jung – he was an intelligent and talented psychiatrist. He was also young, healthy, and energetic. People found him charismatic. His career was going places, and many believed he would succeed to the Chair of Psychiatry at the University of Zürich when it became vacant. Jung also had connections with important psychiatrists, such as

Bleuler at the Burghölzi Clinic, who were potential standard bearers for the Freudian movement. In short, Jung seemed to possess the ideal qualifications to make Freud's psychoanalysis the movement at the forefront of psychotherapy. There was only one problem. Jung's ideas were becoming increasingly less Freudian.

symbols of transformation

Jung was a prolific writer who had already published enough material on psychiatry and Freudian psychoanalysis to fill the first four volumes of his *Collected Works*. In 1911 and 1912, Jung published what was to become the fifth volume, *Symbols of Transformation*. Jung wrote the book in a poetic frenzy, swept along by his insights into the world's myths. He perceived that in all times and places humankind had engaged in the spiritual quest. This was the most powerful human urge of all – to be at one with the Divine Self within.

Jung sent a copy of *Symbols of Transformation* to Freud with trepidation since he knew their differences. Jung believed that it was a search for meaning, not a satisfaction of sexuality, that was the most powerful motivating force for humans; our spiritual urges are as strong as our physical urges. Jung saw myth and religion as signposts to psychological and spiritual truth. Freud saw them as childish delusions that could and should be outgrown. Now Freud's "Crown Prince" was spurning rationalism and espousing the spiritual quest as the goal of life. Freud's reaction was all that Jung feared. He was horrified. Jung was ejected from the Freudian community and, in 1913,

Freud and Jung (both in the center of the picture) | surrounded by medical colleagues in 1911.

1 January 3, 1913 letter in *The Freud/Jung Letters*, ed. William McGuire (New York: Penguin Books, 1991), 295.
2 C. G. Jung, *The Collected Works of C. G. Jung*, vol 5, *Symbols of Transformation*. 2d ed. (London: Routledge & Kegan Paul, 1967), 384.

When Jung was writing *Symbols of Transformation*, he began to realize the importance of myths and of the vital need we all have to reach the inner Divine.

the personal and professional relationship between the two men came to an end. They never met again.

Jung's break with Freud left him in a void. As Freud's disciple, Jung had been made heir of the new psychoanalytic movement. Jung had already given up his hospital post at the Burghölzi Clinic in order to devote himself to promoting psychoanalysis. In 1914 he discontinued lecturing at the University of Zürich. He was now a self-employed analyst without a university, hospital, or the Freudian movement. Jung focused on his private practice and research. Later, he became a professor at the Swiss Federal Institute of Technology in Zurich.

[3] *Memories, Dreams, Reflections*, 164.

freud despairs of jung

Freud had always had some reservations about Jung. He thought the younger man brilliant but flawed. When Jung sent Freud a copy of his work *Symbols of Transformation*, it marked a turning point in their relationship. Freud felt they could no longer associate with one another as their ideas were too different.

> I propose that we abandon our personal relations entirely. I shall lose nothing by it, for my only emotional tie with you has long been a thin thread — the lingering effect of past disappointments. [1]

Could Freud have read a hidden symbolism into passages of Jung's book, *Symbols of Transformation*? He suspected that Jung harbored a symbolic "death wish" toward him — a wish to usurp him as the acknowledged leader of psychoanalysis — and he may have reacted badly to Jung's ideas such as those shown in this quotation: "the god-hero symbolized by the spring zodian (Aries, Taurus) having passed beyond the summer solstice is himself overcome as if by an unconscious longing for death." [2]

However, at about the same time Jung wrote the following: "I wanted at all costs to be able to work with Freud… I had no reason for wishing him dead." [3] We know that one reason for their parting was Jung's belief that Freud's concept of sexual energy needs to include a spiritual dimension. Given that Jung was moving more toward a psychology that dealt with myth, symbol, and spirit, it was inevitable that his path could no longer cross Freud's without difficulties arising.

jung's persona

When Jung broke with Freud in 1913, he was 38. What manner of man was he in midlife? His image, or Persona, was that of a successful doctor, scientist, and university professor, but he also served as a Captain in the Swiss army. One friend recalled he seemed more like a soldier than a therapist.

Jung once told Laurens van der Post, mentor to Britain's Prince of Wales, that it was his enormous physical stamina that enabled him to get through the psychological crisis that followed his break with Freud. Physically, Jung was tall, well-built, fit, handsome, intelligent, striking, and charismatic. As an antidote to his therapy and writing, he was active and energetic. He owned a boat that he often sailed on Lake Zürich in both good and rough weather, and he also went for long walks with his children in the beautiful Swiss mountains.

Spiritual advisor to the Prince of Wales, Sir Laurens van der Post was a friend and admirer of Jung's.

An attractive feature of Jung's personality was his great gift for communicating. Men and women, rich and poor, academics, therapists, and students, all felt at ease with Jung. The village postman attempted Jung's complex volume *Psychology and Alchemy*, which is beyond the capabilities of many postgraduates, because he was inspired by the man who wrote it. A British student commented how apprehensive she was about meeting such a famous person, but as soon as she entered his presence she felt completely at ease. This was what made him such a good therapist.

Jung believed that each one of us has a Persona (who we appear to be) and an Ego (who we consciously think we are). Jung had a strong Ego. This gave him the courage of his convictions. Otherwise, as a young doctor, he would not have refused the career path his university professors mapped out for him. Nor, later, we speculate, would he have left his

A view of the spectacular Swiss scenery that Jung liked to explore with his family.

He tried to get away from the demands of his work and to enjoy the natural world.

the death of Jung's heroic attitude

In December 1913, Jung had a particularly significant dream. He was standing on a rocky mountain with a brown-skinned man. It was the cold hour just before dawn and the stars were fading. The eastern sky began to redden with the rising sun. Suddenly there was a sound – a blast of a hunting horn. Jung immediately recognized it be the horn of Siegfried, a mythological German warrior hero. As the first rays of sun lit the mountain crest, Siegfried appeared in a chariot riding down the mountain slope. Jung knew at once that he had to kill him. With the help of the brown-skinned man, Jung shot Siegfried dead. Jung was shocked by this violent dream. He felt that the hero Siegfried had signified a part of himself and that that part of him had died. It had. It had symbolized the egoistic wish to be head of the psychoanalytic movement. This wish had been undermined by his deeper Self, which had engaged the help of the brown-skinned man that represented his Shadow. His Self was demanding that he abandon all types of worldly ambition to make a long journey, deep into his own psyche.

This is the hero Siegfried, who symbolized for Jung the egoistic part of himself that had to die in order for him to continue his deeper journey.

psychiatric career at the Bughölzi Clinic to promote psychoanalysis. As Freud's "heir," he could have suppressed his misgivings and maintained his status in the Freudian movement, but something within him precipitated the break. Jung did not find the transition easy. He now had no role or status to fall back on. Where was he going?

what is the persona?

the masks we wear

We all have an image that we present to the world. This image is what Jung calls the Persona. "Personas" were the masks once used by ancient Greek actors in their plays, so the audience could immediately see what role they were assuming.

The way we dress, how we speak, the accent we use, the personality that we like to project – all these are part of a Persona that we develop from our earliest years. The Persona is influenced by upbringing; our families, schools, friends, advertisers, culture, and society have norms, values, and attributes that they expect us to accept as desirable and make our own. Personas can be useful. The way we present ourselves tells people a lot about us and helps them react to us in an appropriate way. Personas oil the social wheels and tell us what we can expect from each other. Some people have one image, while others have many that they vary in different situations.

Greek actors held masks up in front of their faces to show the audience which role they were playing.

Both Marilyn Monroe and Elvis Presley felt the strain of being in the public eye.

believing our own propaganda

One danger of the Persona is that we can end up believing our own propaganda. This is a particular problem for those in the media and public eye, who can come to believe they really are the images their public relations staff (PR) have created. Politicians, models, and actors all have a set of expectations placed upon them by their public, PR, and managers about how they should look and behave. If they are not allowed time out to be themselves, the strain of playing a role that is only part of them can be too great. Then there is a danger that the personality can experience total collapse.

We all have many different roles in society and, within each one, people expect certain things from us. This woman is a mother, wife, doctor, and friend and must balance all the demands and expectations each role puts on her.

the real me

The Persona is not "the real me," but rather it is society's expectation of how someone who plays our particular role in society should dress, speak, and behave. If we enter a profession such as medicine, which requires us to be calm, competent, concerned but detached, rational, and always in control, we may end up trying to be this paragon of hospital virtue all day and every day. We can then easily forget to express other parts of our personality that are equally important to us, but which are not compatible with our professional persona. This could be anything from the creative, forgetful, sloppy, imaginative, or sexual side of our being.

identifying with the persona

If we become too concerned about our Personas, we can end up living out the expectations of parents, our ethnic or religious group, or our partners; but we may not be being true to ourselves. We might be living someone else's idea of how our lives should be. If we become too closely identified with our Persona, we can lose bits of ourselves – but not completely. Unfulfilled parts of our personality emerge in dream, fantasy, and through slips of the tongue. If something is forced down into the unconscious, it will strive to get out. If our Persona is too much of a distortion of our real personality, we may find ourselves plagued by strange symptoms, or neuroses.

what is the ego?

who am I?

The Ego is what we think we are. It is our personality as we ourselves consciously know it. It is part of our driving force, our personal desire for self-expression and control over the world around us.

The word "Ego" has many negative connotations. Ego does not mean egotistical or egocentric; ego is a Latin word meaning "I." We develop our sense of "I"-ness in childhood. We hear others describe our personality and behavior, and internalize these descriptions into what we think of as "I." "Michael has a bad temper." "Anna is very cooperative." "Mario is a kind boy." All these labels become part of our identity, but they may be slightly off beam. They may be completely wrong. They are filtered to us through other people's personalities, who interpret our actions according to their own scheme of things and may influence our Ego.

To show that they recognize that only Allah is perfect, Islamic carpet weavers always include a mistake in every one of their carpet designs.

ego deflation

Ego deflation occurs when those around us make us feel inferior because we cannot live up to their high expectations, or because they are jealous of us, or they are incapable of love. If this happens to us when we are children, we may learn to form relationships that force us to give up our own Ego identity.

ego inflation

The other extreme is ego inflation. We may be given exaggerated ideas about our talents and capabilities by those around us. Again, in childhood, this may be because our parents have Egos that need to feel their child is more intelligent, good-looking, and successful than anyone else's. This means that we will grow up thinking that in order to be worthy of love we have to be better than everyone else.

chief executive

The Ego is the Chief Executive of the personality. Like any Chief Executive, it can be demanding. We absorb standards, expectations, goals, and aims. These help us strive to fulfill our potential; but where parents or others have been overdemanding, we may have an Ego that does not allow us to be less than perfect. Getting things wrong and admitting it is part of growing up. Islamic carpet weavers always make one mistake when they knot their threads, because only Allah is perfect. To have a solid Ego identity, we need to learn that we do not have to be perfect. When we accept this as fact, we can start to like ourselves. We can also start to like others. Wholeness is a better goal.

Our ego is what we mean when we say
"I," and it reflects what others think of us
as well as how we feel about ourselves.

understanding ourselves

To understand the Ego needs of others, we must first understand ourselves. We cannot make successful relationships as friends, lovers, or parents unless we have a realistic sense of our own identity. If we know who we ourselves are, we can make better relationship choices.

valuing others

When we feel secure within ourselves, we feel secure in letting partners and children blossom and grow. If we are insecure, we will want to keep them exactly the way they are. We then know what to expect. The Ego is not good at accepting change. It likes to be in control of the situation, which is not possible if the situation is fluid and evolving. Developing a harmonious relationship with our Ego and others means letting go of the need for control. We come to the realization that life is full of the unexpected and that change and growth are good.

relationships

When we operate solely from an Ego basis, we cannot have full and authentic relationships with others because there are barriers of mistrust between us and

woman and ego

Traditionally, Western society taught men to develop a stronger sense of Ego identity than women. We encouraged men to fulfill their potential and to realize their goals and ambitions. We taught women to accommodate themselves to men and to children and to give up their own identities in favor of the Persona of wife and mother. Women were encouraged to become servers and helpmates. Serving others is important and an expression of our love and respect for those around us, but it is important that we are also aware of our own needs. For many women, the last few decades have been a time of self-discovery when they have at last begun to explore their true potential as women. Relationships and parenting can be an important part of this; but alone they will not give us a whole sense of identity. Having a strong Ego means having a strong sense of who we are and what we want to accomplish in life. It means learning to like and to value "me" rather than looking to others for acceptance.

A strong Ego helps women to love and value themselves as they truly are.

them. The Ego makes us compete, to be better, bigger, and stronger than other people. Others' success makes us jealous, rather than joyful. Alternatively, if we do not have a strong Ego, we may form damaging relationships. We may allow someone with a much stronger sense of personal identity to run our lives for us. This can be disastrous, especially if they do not want us to grow into our true identity. We may find ourselves in a relationship that traps us into being the man or woman they want us to be and not ourselves.

Our relationships are always affected by the two Egos involved. Couples may be very different characters but balance one another well.

We need to know ourselves and our own goals and objectives in life. We can then enter into an equal partnership with someone else as two strong people who have decided to make life's journey together. We can then form meaningful and generous relationships in which both parties evolve.

identifying persona and ego

mirrors exercise

For this exercise, you need somewhere you can sit undisturbed. The exercise is in two stages. Do the first stage, which will take about twenty minutes, one evening and the second stage, which will take one to two hours, the next evening. You will need some sheets of plain paper and a pen. For the second stage you will also need colored pens or pencils.

the first day

1   On a sheet of paper, draw a circle and write in the center of it: "Positive mirror: what I like about myself."

2   Relax for a few minutes and think about all the nice things you have done for people. Think about those who like and love you and what they might say about you. Now think about what you might say about yourself. It is your view of your positive qualities that is important. Write down all the characteristics that you like. Now leave the list until tomorrow.

3   Next morning note any dreams that came to you during the night. There may be messages about your self-image in them.

It is good to consider what others like about your personality, but the most important element of this exercise is what *you* like about yourself.

the second day

1   Take a sheet of paper and your colored pens. Relax and close your eyes. Allow an image to form in your mind's eye of "The positive me." See if you can name this image of yourself. Now draw it.

2   Relax again and close your eyes. Allow an image to form in your mind's eye of "Myself as others would like me to be," possibly a contrast to you as you really are. This is a Persona others would like you to adopt. See if you can name this image. Now draw it. You may find that more that one image comes to mind. Maybe the expectations of your manager are different from those of your partner, parents, children, or friends. If so, draw all these images.

3   Finally, form in your mind's eye a realistic image of "Me as I would like to be." Draw the image and write down any thoughts or feelings that you have about it. Name it if you can.

4   On a new sheet of paper, draw a circle and write in the center: "Mirror 2: the image I present to others." Look at the images you have drawn – your positive image, others' images of you, and the "real you." Are there differences between them? Do you project yourself differently to others from the way you feel you are? What positive aspects of yourself are you hiding? Why? Are others' expectations limiting you in some way?

5   On Mirror 2, write down a list of qualities that describes the way you present yourself to others. Compare it with the list of qualities that you wrote on your positive mirror. What differences are there?

Having completed the exercise, look at the image of the real you once more.

Writing and drawing images of how others see you can help you distinguish those images and the person you want to be.

personality types

With the publication of his study of mythology, Symbols of Transformation, Jung was marking the territory that was to become his own. His fame began to spread, but all was not well with the world. In 1913, as he reached midlife, Jung had some powerful and frightening visions. They seemed to portend a terrible international crisis.

In 1914, the madness of World War I was unleashed, engulfing Europe and dragging other nations in behind it. Switzerland was a neutral country isolated behind its impenetrable mountains, but it had to prepare itself for possible attack. There was much deprivation, and food was in short supply. However, the war did not stop the stream of famous foreign visitors who traveled to see Jung.

Edith Rockefeller was one of the world's wealthiest women with a fortune of $100 million dollars. She was giving financial support to the impoverished Irish writer, James Joyce. Joyce's most famous novel is *Ulysses*. Ironically, this is the Latin version of the name of the ancient Greek mythological hero, Odysseus, whose journey into the underworld Jung was to take as a model for his own psychological journey. Edith Rockefeller thought Joyce had a number of problems, and she was eager for him to be treated by Carl Jung. Joyce, however, would rather have a few shots of whiskey than undergo psychotherapy.

Joyce did actually return to Jung with his disturbed daughter, after trying twenty other psychiatrists without success, but he did not like the diagnosis. Jung felt that the intense relationship between Joyce and Lucia was an obstacle to her treatment. He indicated that Joyce was projecting his own inner feminine, his Anima, onto his daughter. Joyce believed his daughter's poetry was a new art form and that she had the gift of "Celtic clairvoyance." Jung explained that Lucia's poems indicated latent schizophrenia. Joyce was convinced that Jung was a philistine who could not appreciate his daughter's gifts. The treatment came to an abrupt end.

Despite Joyce's skepticism, many creative people were attracted to Jung's approach, which worked through symbolism and the world of the imagination. The great German novelist Herman Hesse had analysis with Jung. Jung's idea of individuation became the motif of Hesse's novel *Demian*, and Jung's type theory underpinned *Narziss und Goldmund*.

The Unfolding by Rassouli. During World War I, Jung encountered many psychological problems among the soldiers he treated. He was also in deep crisis within his own psyche.

the war years

Jung did not spend the whole of World War I in private practice. He was drafted to serve as an army doctor and found himself dealing with typical army problems – sexual diseases and bad feet. However, his psychiatric and language skills were soon recognized, and he was given a more demanding role.

Swiss neutrality obliged the Swiss to intern any personnel from either side of the conflict who crossed their frontier to evade capture by the enemy. Jung was made commandant of an internment camp for British officers, soldiers, and civilian merchant seamen. This might seem a strange job for a psychiatrist, but the men's main problems were psychological. They were trapped in a neutral country as noncombatants, when over the Swiss border in France and Germany, their comrades were still fighting and dying. Jung did much to improve conditions. He pressed the British government for the civilian seaman to receive pay and encouraged officers to attend university courses to alleviate the mind-numbing boredom. Outwardly, Jung seemed to be coping with the emotional hurt of his break with Freud. Inwardly, under the veneer of the professional persona, he was in deep psychological crisis. His previous Ego had been symbolically destroyed in his 1913 "Siegfried" dream. Now new forces were released in him.

World War I had an enormous effect on everyone, and Jung, as an army doctor, saw the psychological scars first hand. He did much to alleviate soldiers' problems as he encountered them.

The symbolism of the sea, lakes, and running water was always important for Jung. Water is generally associated with the unconscious, and indeed Jung always preferred to live near water. It seemed he was most able to access his own feelings there. In August 1913, Jung took his childhood friend, Albert Oeri, and three other men on a four-day sailing trip in his boat on Lake Zürich. Albert Oeri read the adventures of the ancient Greek hero, Odysseus, to them. One of the stories is the Nekyia, or Night-Sea Journey. This describes Odysseus' descent into the Underworld, the realm of the dead. The term "Nekyia" captured Jung's imagination. He used it to describe the major life transition he was entering as he began an inner journey into the unconscious.

journey of exploration

Jung's break with Freud precipitated a psychological crisis. He felt like a small sailing boat cut adrift on storm-tossed waters. Images, symbols, and strange mythological figures flooded his dreams and preoccupied his waking hours. He could not escape them. The only thing to do was to face them. Like a mariner deciding to sail into the face of the storm, Jung plunged into the turbulent sea of the unconscious. He began a five year period where he recorded every dream, daydream, and vision. He entered into interior dialogue with the people he found there and rigorously analyzed the symbolism that appeared. The process worked. As the War ended in 1918, so too did Jung's Nekyia.

He emerged immeasurably stronger, with insights into the structure of the psyche that would be the foundation of his psychology. He also introduced something new. His experience convinced him that analysts should undergo analysis before starting training. This might seem obvious to us now, but originally all analysts were medical doctors. In medicine, it is not considered necessary to experience a disease in order to treat it.

Directly after Jung's break with Freud, he knew he had to face the storm brewing in his unconscious, even though there was a danger it could overwhelm him.

in britain

Jung's stint as commander of the internment camp confirmed his liking for the British. Like the Americans, they seemed to him rugged individualists compared with the conformist Swiss. The admiration was mutual; the British liked him. Even the dour Scottish psychologist William McDougall once remarked that, because of Jung, Switzerland finally had a justifiable reason for existing.

ghosts

In 1920, Jung was invited to Britain to give seminars. In his leisure time, he visited Tintagel Castle, the supposed birthplace of King Arthur, and mystical Glastonbury where St. Joseph of Arimathea is reputed to have brought the Holy Grail for safekeeping. Jung's intuitive mind had been open to the paranormal from a very early age. He had experienced many phenomena in Switzerland, and here he was in a land steeped in history — and in ghosts.

Jung disliked hotels, so he asked a friend to help him rent a cheap country cottage where he could stay at the weekends. However, when he was at the cottage, he got little rest. On the first weekend, he woke to find a sickly, cancerous smell pervading the

intuitive thinkers

Jung was aware of seeking God from his earliest years. He once wrote to a young clergyman that all his thoughts circled around God like planets and were irresistibly drawn to him. Often he felt the promptings of divine will in his life and felt compelled to follow it wherever it took him. Like many who make innovative discoveries, his mind was visual. Ideas often came first in image and symbol.

Jung liked nothing better than discussions with quantum physicists, such as Einstein, Wolfgang Pauli, and Werner Heisenberg, whose minds also transcended linear thought to be more intuitive thinkers. In his years with Freud, Jung's intuitive spiritual side conflicted with his intellectual and scientific side. Freud was a rational materialist determined to make psychoanalysis a science. He did not want psychoanalysis' image tainted by contact with anything "odd." For Freud, Jung-the-mystic could not simultaneously be Jung-

the-scientist. Now, as he emerged from his mid-life crisis, Jung's intuition and thinking had begun to integrate. From this integration came his most powerful work.

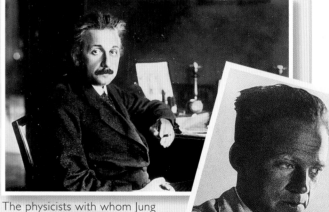

The physicists with whom Jung enjoyed conversing included Einstein (above) and Heinsenburg (right).

In Britain Jung visited Tintagel Castle, the reputed | birthplace of King Arthur and a place steeped in myth.

bedroom. The next weekend the smell was accompanied by a rustling noise and something brushing along the walls. It seemed to Jung that a large animal must be in the room. However, on the third weekend, there were knocking sounds. By now, most people would have given up and decided to spend their weekends elsewhere, but not Jung. On the fifth weekend, he woke up to find a hideous apparition beside him on the pillow. It was an old woman, part of whose face was missing.

Jung questioned the cleaners, who confirmed that the cottage was indeed haunted. This explained the suspiciously low rent and the cleaners' reluctance to be there after dark. Not all of Jung's colleagues were inclined to believe in ghosts. The colleague who had rented the cottage on Jung's behalf was unimpressed with what Jung told him, so Jung challenged him to spend the night there. He tried, but was so terrified he did not even remain in the bedroom. He took his bed into the garden and slept outside with his shotgun beside him. Shortly afterward, the cottage's owner had it demolished – it was impossible for anyone to live there.

thinking on personality types

One of Jung's aims during his British seminars in 1920 was to refine his ideas about personality. In 1921 he published what is now the sixth volume of his *Collected Works*, *Psychological Types*. In addition to two attitudes to the world, extroversion and introversion, Jung identified four personality types or functions.

ancient ideas about personality

The idea that there are four basic personality types is found in many cultures and is at the heart of astrology. The ancient Greeks believed that the whole of creation was made up of four elements – Earth, Air, Fire, and Water. Different substances were made up of different combinations of these four elements. Personality was seen as influenced by these four elements – people were a mixture of the elements, but in each of us one element would predominate. This would affect our personality type and also our body type and therefore the types of disease we would be susceptible to. In astrology, the Air signs are Aquarius, Gemini, and Libra. The Fire signs are Aries, Leo, and Sagittarius. The Water signs are Pisces, Cancer, and Scorpio. The Earth signs are Taurus, Virgo, and Capricorn.

Examples of the four different personality types (from left to right): Earth-type woman; Air-type man; Fire-type woman; and Water-type man.

"For complete orientation all four functions should contribute equally: thinking should facilitate cognition and judgement, feeling should tell us how and to what extent a thing is important or unimportant for us, sensation should convey concrete reality to us through seeing, hearing, tasting, etc, and intuition should enable us to divine the hidden possibilities in the background, since these too belong to the complete picture of a given situation." [1]

astrology and personality type

Jung called his four personality types "sensation," "intuition," "thinking," and "feeling." They relate to the four elements: sensation with Earth, thinking with Air, intuition with Fire, and feeling with Water. The idea that intuition is fiery can seem strange, but if you think of Jung's idea of intuition as akin to creative inspiration, then it begins to make sense.

At that time in Europe, astrology was a subject of serious study. If a patient was particularly difficult to understand, Jung would send him or her to an expert astrologer to have a natal chart prepared, which Jung would then interpret psychologically. There is no simple relationship between sun sign and dominant personality type, but a skilled astrologer can predict the dominant personality type from the overall dynamics of the chart. Jung himself did not believe that the Sun sign was the most important aspect of an astrological chart. He was more interested in seasonal and planetary influences.

four functions

In order to function in the world, we need to receive information and then make judgments about how to act upon it. Sensation and intuition are different ways of perceiving and receiving information. Thinking and feeling are judging functions. They are two different measuring instruments that help us to process the information we receive.

We cannot use two perceptual functions at the same time. The different modes of perceiving, sensation, and intuition are like looking at the world through different pairs of glasses with different lenses. We can only use one pair at a time, and what we perceive when we use our sensation function will be different from what we perceive when we use our intuition. Our personality type will incline us to use one function more readily than the other. We will use one of the perceptual modes, either sensation or intuition, as our main information source. We call upon the other mode when we need to, but it is less familiar to us and therefore we use it less skillfully. Similarly, we cannot use two judgmental functions as measuring instruments. We use either thinking or feeling first to evaluate the data we receive. We may then call upon the other judgmental function for extra information.

[1] C. G. Jung, *The Collected Works of C. G. Jung,* vol. 6, *Psychological Types.* 2d ed. (London: Routledge & Kegan Paul, 1971), 518.

understanding personality types

Jung's ideas on personality types are clearly illustrated in the original Star Trek series. Here, Mr. Spock was the thinker and Bones, Dr. McCoy, the feeler. Scotty was the sensate engineer and Captain Kirk the intuitive leader. Captain Kirk's impulsiveness was always getting them into trouble, but his leaps of lateral imagination got them out of them again. When the team worked well together, they solved most of their problems.

Each of these personality types is also affected by whether the individual is an introvert or extrovert.

sensation

Sensation operates through the physical senses, and we use it to discover facts. Sensation types are usually practical people who spot physical clues that others miss. As doctors, they make good diagnosticians. As mechanics, they will often recognize the annoying engine noise that electronic fault-finding devices failed to identify. As fashion experts, they match color with an unerring eye. Sensation is reality-oriented and focused in the here and now. Sensate people remember names and dates and make great collectors, whether of stamps or antiques. Introverted sensation people appreciate esthetics and may be skilled artists or musicians.

intuition

Intuition shows us meanings and implications. It tells us how situations are likely to develop in the future. Intuitives have hunches and "know" things, but do not know how they know. Intuition is the function of

Star Trek used very clear personality types, with the intuitive Captain Kirk as the leader of the crew.

the imagination. People with extroverted intuition have an idea where society is going and will be at the leading edge of new technologies, businesses, fashions, and creeds. They love new ideas and new projects. Introverted intuition is the function of the creative writer – and of the daydreamer. Intuitives can be content to dream their lives away without ever bringing their brilliant imaginings into fruition. Intuitives start more than they finish.

thinking

Thinking tells us whether something is logical and rational, correct or incorrect. Thinking types enjoy analyzing information and making logical decisions. They tend to be good at science, mathematics, or business. Introverted thinking people like computers and classification systems. They can be good at playing the stock market and gambling. Extroverted thinkers love to organize others. They are born administrators.

feeling

Feeling tells us whether something is pleasant or unpleasant, good or bad, helpful or harmful. We need our feeling function when dealing with people and making relationships. Feeling people make good social workers and will move heaven and earth to help a deserving client. Therapists need a well-developed feeling function in order to value and understand their clients. Feeling people build relationships of trust and are excellent parents, teachers, and ministers.

developing our functions

In childhood, we naturally prefer one function. In adolescence we begin to develop a second function. Later in adulthood we begin to develop our third function, but this will remain somewhere in the background. Few people develop their fourth function fully. The fourth function is a "shadow" function.

Our personality type affects the type of jobs to which we are drawn. Sensation types make good mechanics, while introverted sensate people may become artists (below left). Extroverted intuitives are interested in new technology (below center). The scientist here is a "thinker," while the teacher (below right) is more of a feeling person.

dominant and secondary functions

Our dominant and secondary functions are the perceptual function and the judgmental function that we most use in everyday life. These functions impact on our outer personality. They affect how people see us and react to us. They can also indicate the type of work that will suit us best.

sensation with thinking or feeling

Sensation and thinking operate well together in the word of business. Many accountants are introverted sensate thinkers. They are careful and meticulous. Extroverted sensate thinkers like to be active. They enjoy getting out of the office and working outdoors in jobs that require a logical approach. Farming, construction, the police, the military, and security work appeal. Sensate feeling types are particularly people-oriented and tactile. They enjoy customer service jobs and also excel at physically caring for others, so health-care jobs, sales, childcare, catering, entertainment, and the leisure industries can appeal.

intuition with thinking or feeling

Intuitive thinkers like ideas and creating new systems. Academia and information technology can appeal. Introverted intuitives who are also deep thinkers can became inventors, taking science beyond the contemporary boundaries. Unfortunately, their ideas may be so advanced that they are dismissed as crackpot by their own generation. Extroverted intuitive thinkers enjoy the cut and thrust of business and management consultancy. Introverted intuitive feelers make excellent therapists and predominate in religious work. Extroverted intuitive feelers are often found in the media and advertising.

Extroverted sensate thinkers are extremely active and enjoy working outdoors.

relating to opposites

Relating to a person whose first and second functions are opposite to ours can create problems. Sensate thinkers are interested in practical matters, business, and politics. They will be easily bored by discussions about people's feelings. Intuitive feelers are romantic. They like being told that their partner loves them. "Of course I love you," the sensate thinker replies. "I bought you that new CD player, didn't I?" Intuitive thinkers talk about abstract ideas and find sensate feelers materialist. A sensate feeling parent may feel hurt by an intuitive thinking child's apparent coldness. When she or he is in the middle of doing something complex on the computer, an intuitive thinker may find it irritating to feel obliged to respond to a sensate feeling person's need for hugs. This does not make these relationships impossible, but it does make them harder.

Encouraging one another is very important. Here, a sensate wife is involving her husband in the decisions about decorations in their home, while the intuitive feeling mother helps her son with his homework.

partnership

A relationship where we have the same pattern of functions as our partner can be too much of a good thing. But if we have one function that is a common denominator, we have a basis of understanding from which to enjoy our differences. An intuitive thinker and an intuitive feeler will stimulate one another's imagination and provoke new ideas. The feeler will encourage the thinker to express his or her feelings, and the thinker will encourage the feeler to set goals for self-improvement. Similarly, a sensate thinker and a sensate feeler can share an interest in sensuality, enjoyment of good food, and beautiful surroundings. From this base, they can encourage each other to grow.

thinking or feeling?

The chart below contains some statements that will help you to discover which judgmental function you use most. However, you should remember that a short test cannot be totally definitive. Your responses will give you an indication of your type preference but you can also read the descriptions on the previous pages to decide which one matches your personality best.

As you look through the statements below, check yes or no in the relevant column or, alternatively, write down the numbers of any phrases that you answer yes to on a separate sheet of paper. Make a note of your positive answers and then refer to the section "analyzing your scores" on the opposite page to see whether your thinking or feeling function is the more dominant.

Are you the type that analyzes and looks on, or the type that empathizes and joins in?

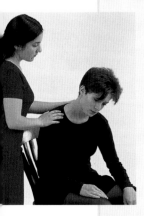

		yes	no
1	I enjoy debate and intellectual argument.		
2	I prefer reading novels with happy endings.		
3	I find it easy to compliment people.		
4	I like to be thought of as warmhearted.		
5	Emotional displays are irritating.		
6	I like to be thought of as kind.		
7	I usually keep my feelings to myself.		
8	I wish people were more emotionally expressive.		
9	I am a very rational person.		
10	People often see me as detached.		
11	I am very sensitive and empathize with the world's suffering.		
12	I enjoy reading about scientific advances.		
13	Friends tell me their problems because I can analyze them.		
14	Friends tell me their problems because they value my sympathy.		
15	I enjoy jobs that involve helping people.		
16	I enjoy jobs that involve dealing with systems.		
17	I am sometimes accused of being overcritical.		
18	I am more interested in people than the average person.		
19	I find it difficult to criticize people.		
20	I am firm but fair in my dealings with people.		

analyzing your scores

Now that you have finished reading through the chart, take a look at your responses. If you have more "Yeses" for questions 1, 5, 7, 9, 10, 12, 13, 16, 17, and 20, your thinking function is likely to be stronger than your feeling side. If you have more "Yeses" for questions 2, 3, 4, 6, 8, 11, 14, 15, 18, and 19, feeling is likely to be stronger than thinking.

If you score equally, you should take a look at the descriptions of the functions again on pages 62–65 and see if you can spot the one that best describes you. Once you know your stronger function, you can then balance its extremes by learning to cultivate and make use of your weaker function. The two boxes below give you some ideas to help you achieve this important balance.

This manager is a "thinker." This means she is likely to launch straight into her criticisms when talking to staff, so she must learn to offer encouragement first.

balancing feeling with thinking

Feeling people want to be liked. This can make being a manager particularly difficult since you find it much easier to praise than to criticize. As a teacher, you are tempted to give high marks for effort, even if the work is not very good. You need to rely on your own evaluation of yourself rather than deriving your self-esteem from what others think about you. You may even be loyal to others when they are seriously in the wrong, so avoid getting into situations that you feel uncomfortable about because you feel pressured by someone close to you.

balancing thinking with feeling

Thinking people need to consider others' feelings. When you implement change at work, make sure you explain why. Take notice of people's reactions and try to involve them in some way. Check your partner's and coworkers' feelings on a regular basis. Make sure they do not misinterpret your preoccupation with your work or other interests as a lack of interest in them. Remember to praise staff and children before you offer helpful advice about where they are going wrong. At least once a week, tell your partner and children that you love them.

sensation or intuition?

The chart below contains some statements to help you discover the perceptual function you use the most. Again, you should remember that your responses will indicate your type preference, but you should also read the descriptions on the previous pages to see which resonates with you. See which of these questions you answer "yes" to and either check the relevant boxes, or make a note of your positive answers on a separate sheet of paper. Once you have done this, refer to the "analyzing your scores" section to see whether your sensation function is more dominant than your intuition, or vice versa.

		yes	no
1	Once I have found my way somewhere, I can remember how to get there again.		
2	I mean to replace missing buttons immediately, but rarely do.		
3	My desk or work station is always neat and tidy.		
4	I often make factual errors.		
5	I can spend hours fantasizing about things.		
6	People who go into great detail are boring.		
7	I always put tools and equipment back in their right place when I finish a job.		
8	I usually know exactly what I am going to do each week.		
9	I have had a number of changes of career.		
10	When using a new piece of equipment, I read the instructions first.		
11	I nearly always eat meals at regular times.		
12	I am always trying out new ways of doing things.		
13	I have hundreds of ideas – too many to put into practice.		
14	I can complete most of my plans and projects.		
15	People know I have my feet on the ground.		
16	I tend to do too many things at once.		
17	I sometimes exaggerate to make a story more interesting.		
18	I relay the facts exactly as they are.		
19	I usually know how long jobs will take.		
20	I often underestimate the time it takes to do something.		

You may always clear your desk at the end of the day, or it may be a new habit that you need to form.

balancing intuition with sensation

If your intuition is stronger than your sensation, once a week do something practical that you have been putting off. Sew the button on that coat that you never wear because the button is missing. Clear your desk. Go for the dental check-up that you have been avoiding for months. Get the mechanic to listen to that odd engine noise that you have been meaning to do something about. Neglected tasks absorb some of our unconscious energy. When we clear away jobs that we have been putting off, we feel lighter and ready to enjoy ourselves or to get something else done that we really enjoy.

analyzing your scores

If you have answered "Yes" to questions 1, 3, 7, 8, 10, 11, 14, 15, 18, and 19, your sensation function is likely to be stronger than your intuition. If you have predominantly "Yes" answers for questions 2, 4, 5, 6, 9, 12, 13, 16, 17, and 20, your intuition seems stronger than your sensation. If you score equally, then look at the descriptions of the functions again and see if you can spot which best matches you.

balancing sensation with intuition

Sensation types tend to do things the same way they have always done them. You can develop strong habits about what you eat, wear, and read, and where you go for vacations and leisure. There is nothing wrong with this, but try once a week to do something you have never done before. Drive a different route to work, try a different restaurant, buy something – a magazine, lipstick color, or whatever – that you have never bought before. When we introduce small changes in our lives, they stimulate the imagination and broaden our outlook.

If you have not been wearing your favorite shirt because it is missing a button, take time to sew it back on!

anima and goddess

> Jung the intuitive thinker was highly attracted to intuitive women who could both share his intellectual interests and help him expand his horizons to go beyond the confines of a materialistic male-dominated medical establishment.

Jung believed that Western society overvalued the masculine at the expense of the feminine. He looked to the twenty-first century to redress the imbalance toward the masculine that he believed had distorted our society and religions. Jung enjoyed the company of women, and pioneer women analysts helped him to develop many of his key ideas. The new profession of psychotherapy attracted many women. As an emerging profession, it was easier for women to enter this field than some more traditionally male-dominated careers. Another attraction was that psychotherapy was a career in which helping the sick and educating people about their feelings were important goals.

Many women became important figures in the Jungian movement around the world. Dr. Beatrice Hinkle, a Jungian analyst in New York, was the first translator of *Symbols of Transformation* and so she introduced America to the first of Jung's work that showed the flowering of this thought after his final break with Freud. Dr. Esther M. Harding, Dr. Kristinne Mann, and Dr. Eleanor Bertine set up Jungian practices in the United States as early as the 1920s. In Zürich, Dr. Marie-Louise von Franz became a leading training analyst and writer, who, along with others, continued Jung's research and training work after his death.

Olga Fröbe-Kapteyn organized the famous Eranos conferences in the 1930s. Olga was a highly-cultured and intellectual Dutch woman whom Jung believed had mediumistic gifts. Her conferences brought together leading scholars in the humanities and sciences. Held at her villa at Ascona on Lake Maggiore in Switzerland, they became annual events at which Jung was able to meet with distinguished scholars to give papers and refine his ideas in a community of leading world authorities in many disciplines. These conferences gave Jung significant platforms from which to develop his teachings.

Celestial Union by Rassouli. Jung believed that is was important to balance the masculine with the feminine. He was sure that the feminine was greatly undervalued and was quick to include women analysts within his own circles.

the women
in jung's life

emma jung

There are no biographies of Carl Jung's wife Emma, but people recalled her as a remarkable woman who was attractive, kind, and gracious. She was also sensitive, introverted, and shy. If she had married a conventional Swiss banker, her life would have been easy. Her fate, however, was to marry a genius.

Carl was convinced as soon as he met Emma that he would marry her. At the time she was only fourteen. Seven years later, on February 14, 1903, they were married and began by moving into the Burghölzi Clinic where Jung's career was really just beginning.

Emma and Carl had five children together; their two eldest daughters, Agathe and Anna, were born on December 26, 1904 and February 8, 1906. A son, Franz, was born on November 28, 1908. By this time, the family needed a larger home. They arranged for a substantial house to be built just outside Zürich at Küsnacht, and in 1909 they moved in. At this time, Carl gave up his hospital post to concentrate on his private practice and his work promoting the Freudian movement. Marianne was born on September 20, 1910.

Carl and Emma in 1903, shortly after their wedding. They began their married life at the Burghölzi Clinic.

Carl seemed not entirely happy about the quick succession of pregnancies. He wrote to Freud in 1911 that he and Emma were trying contraception but knew that an accident might happen. In any event, another daughter, Emma, was born on March 18, 1914.

other women

In early twentieth-century Switzerland, the expected custom was to marry and settle down once a man had a job and income. Jung followed this convention but he did not find it easy. During the first few years of his and Emma's marriage, all was well, but there were great differences between them. Emma Jung had been educated in the literature and arts of her day by tutors at home. This was obviously not an education that would enable her to understand psychiatry and psychotherapy. In this respect, she was like many of her contemporaries, for Swiss women commonly did not attend university. In later years, as her children grew up, Emma trained as an analyst, set up a successful practice, and wrote on Jungian psychology. In the meantime, however, she found herself married to a man who was at the leading edge of the new psychotherapy. He was a voracious reader, prolific writer, and keen researcher. He desperately needed intellectual challenges.

sabina spielrein

One of the first women to be involved with Jung was a young Russian woman, Sabina Spielrein. They first met when she was admitted to the Burghölzi Clinic in 1904 as a patient suffering from hysteria. In Russia, women could attend university. When her crisis was over, Sabina Spielrein became one of the first women to train as a doctor at the University of Zürich. She remained friendly with Jung after she left the clinic, and it was rumored that two years later she became his lover. Their relationship ended in 1909.

toni wolff

Another intellectual woman eventually became Jung's lifelong friend. Antonia (Toni) Wolff was the youngest daughter of a wealthy Zürich family. She became Jung's patient in 1910 after the death of her father propelled her into deep, spiraling depression. However, after successful treatment, she became an analyst in training.

Carl and Emma (third from left) were part of the Third Psychoanalytic Congress in Weimar in 1911. Toni was also present (front row, third from right).

the dark beauty

Toni had dark hair, beautiful bone structure, and fine features. Unlike most of those who came to study as Jungian analysts, she was always elegantly and stylishly dressed. Toni's appearance was attractive to Jung, but that was not all. In Toni, Jung saw a woman of remarkable intellect – a poet with a deep feeling for religion and philosophy.

a mutual attraction

To Toni, Jung was a man in his prime. Not only was he physically attractive to her, he also had a magnetic personality. Furthermore, he was a leading figure in the world of psychoanalysis in which she wished to make her mark and, as a teacher and mentor, he had some elements of the father-figure that she had lost. The attraction was mutual.

Toni Wolff introduced Jung to new aspects of Eastern philosophy and to astrology. She knew how to interpret natal charts. Jung sensed that Freud would not approve and, on May 8 and 12, 1911, he wrote to Freud about it directly:

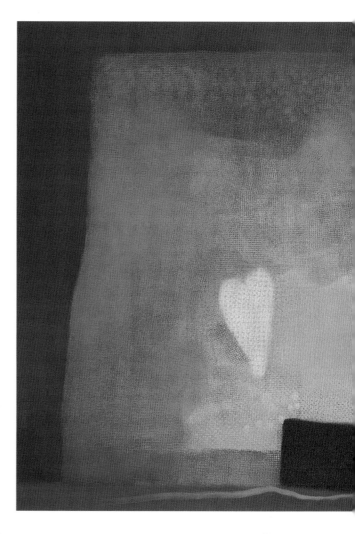

"At the moment I am looking into astrology, which seems indispensable for a proper understanding of mythology. There are strange and wondrous things in these lands of darkness. Please don't worry about my wanderings in these infinitudes. I shall return laden with rich booty for our knowledge of the human psyche. For a while longer I must intoxicate myself on magic perfumes in order to fathom the secrets that lie hidden in the abysses of the unconscious." [1]

[1] *Freud/Jung Letters*, 223.

From the *Hitchcock* series by Robert Natkin. Both Toni and Jung were attracted to one another and, eventually, became lovers. Toni was an important part of Jung's life and joined his family circle for over forty years.

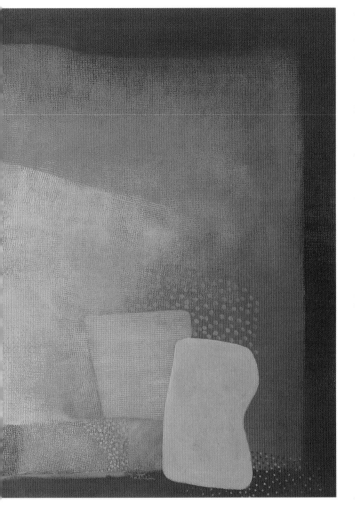

"My evenings are taken up very largely with astrology. I made horoscopic calculations in order to find a clue to the core of psychological truth. Some remarkable things have turned up which will certainly appear incredible to you. For instance, it appears that the signs of the zodiac are character pictures, in other words libido symbols which depict the typical qualities of the libido at a given moment." [2]

helpmate

During 1913, Jung was going into his Nekyia crisis. Toni Wolff could help him interpret the symbols that appeared in his dreams and visions. Jung was often in an extreme state of agitation as mythological image after image welled up from his unconscious and threatened to overwhelm him. Toni encouraged him to persist with the difficult work of analyzing these images. Jung wrote, "I was in effect writing letters to the Anima, that is, to a part of myself with a different viewpoint from my conscious one." [3] At that time Toni came to represent for Jung an important aspect of his Anima, or the vital female component of a man's psyche that guides him to a deeper inner level.

wife and mistress

Around 1915, Emma decided heroically that Carl needed Toni as well as herself. Toni soon became known as his friend and became a recognized part of the Jung family circle. From then on, she was usually a guest at Sunday lunch at Küsnacht. She frequently traveled with Jung to the conferences he attended, with or without Emma. She also spent a great deal of time at the retreat that Jung later built at Bollingen. Toni remained extremely close to Jung until her death in 1955. This relationship, which had a huge impact on Jung, spanned over forty years.

Emma accepted Toni and Carl's relationship and welcomed Toni into the family.

[2] *Freud/Jung Letters*, 226.
[3] *Memories, Dreams, Reflections*, 186.

love, marriage, and family

Jung was very attracted to Toni Wolff, but he had no desire to marry her. For a middle-class Swiss such as Jung, marriage was about being a responsible citizen and raising a family. People were expected to marry "suitable" partners. This meant their partner had to be from a similar background, so that their families got along.

emma and toni

There are hints throughout his writings that Jung saw two different types of women. Some women, he felt, were destined for marriage and children and other

women were muses who inspired men to new potentials. Jung felt that he needed both women in his life in order to function at his best, so Emma, with amazing generosity, arranged their lives so this was possible. This might seem strange to us today, but the idea that men had intellectual needs that were beyond the scope of their wives was not uncommon in early twentieth-century Europe. Shortly before she died, Emma actually commented that she would always be grateful to Toni for doing for her husband what neither she nor anyone else could do at a most critical time. She was referring, of course, to Jung's desperate Nekyia period.

jung's mother

Jung describes his mother as an earthy extrovert in his writings. This might suggest that she was a simple, uncomplicated woman. However, nothing could be farther from the truth. She had a disturbing habit of making statements that seemed to come straight from the unconscious without any conscious censorship. A few days after Jung's father died, his mother suddenly told him, "He died in time for you. You did not understand each other and he might have become a hindrance to you."[1] It is true that the relationship had been a tricky one. Jung's ideas about religion were unlikely to find favor with a father who was a clergyman. However, this was a strange way for a

Jung saw two types of women – those that fulfilled the nurturing role and those that became muses. Emma was the conventional wife and mother.

[1] Jung, C.G. *Memories, Dreams and Reflections*, recorded and edited by Aniela Jaffé and translated by R. and C. Wilson. (Fontana Paperback, 1995 ed.), p 116.

Jung's mother and father, Emilie and Paul. After Paul's death, Emilie continued to be a dominant figure in her son's life, which often caused problems because she did not approve of his choice of profession.

a dual image

During Jung's mother's frequent stays in the hospital when he was a child, he was cared for by the family's maid. She had black hair and olive skin, and seemed to him familiar yet mysterious. He became strongly attached to her. While his mother was away, he also spent time with a pretty, blonde-haired, blue-eyed young woman who took him on outings. This woman was his future mother-in-law, Frau Rauschenbach.

Scientific research shows that men are likely to marry women who physically resemble their mothers. On the surface, Carl's mother was a conventional Swiss-German hausfrau. However, underneath the surface, she was actually a strange medium-type who had tendencies toward psychological illness.

Carl was forever torn between conventional women and unconventional, exotic, otherworldly women. He married the daughter of the conventional blonde-haired woman he had so admired as a young child, and yet he was always attracted to women such as Sabina Spielrein and Toni Wolff. These women were dark-haired and olive-skinned, reminded him of his childhood maid, and had something mysterious and otherworldly about them.

mother to speak to her son about his father, and particularly when it was so soon after his death.

Jung's mother's comments could be crushing, and as she disapproved of his choice of psychiatry as a specialization, she did often hurt Carl deeply. Once, when she visited him at the Burghölzi Clinic, she looked around at the charts that he was using to record patient's reaction times and asked him doubt-fully, "Do those things mean anything?"[2] Jung at once felt his confidence shatter.

[2] Notes from a seminar given in 1928–30 by C. G. Jung, quoted in Frank McLynn, *Carl Gustav Jung* (St. Martin's Press, 1996), 77.

anima

No one is wholly female or wholly male. Within us all is a powerful archetype of the contra-sexual side of our personalities. Jung called the inner feminine of men the Anima and the inner masculine of women the Animus. The more sexually stereotyped our upbringing, the greater the difference between the Anima or Animus and our Persona.

the stages of anima

Jung believed that the Anima developed from three sources – a man's mother, his experiences of women as companions, and his own femininity (female sex hormones are found, to some extent, in every male body). A man's Anima image will depend on his stage of development. Eve is the first Anima stage. She is the Earth Mother, primitive, sexual, unconscious, instinctive, and unthinking. Hers is the sensation function. A goddess such as Aphrodite, Greek goddess of love, or a woman such as Cleopatra, could represent the second stage. This is the lover goddess who enters into a romantic relationship with a man. Hers is the feeling function. At the third and fourth stages, the function of the Anima is not to enter into relationship with a man but to inspire him to greater things. A third stage could be the image of the Virgin Mary where personal love is transformed into spiritual devotion. Hers is the function of intuition. Fourth is the Anima as the personification of Sophia or Wisdom. This relates to the thinking function, but to the intuitive thinking that takes us to the highest realms of spirituality. The brilliantly intellectual Queen Elizabeth I of England was an unobtainable Anima figure for her male courtiers and she was represented in art as Astraea – a star goddess.

Eve is the ultimate, primitive, instinctive Earth mother, and she represents the first stage of the Anima.

The second stage of Anima development for a man involves a lover goddess such as Aphrodite.

projection

If a man is unaware of his Anima, he looks constantly for the perfect woman, one that can embody his Anima image for him. When he finds that his partner is a real person and not an image, the temptation is to move on to search for perfect again. Much first adolescent love is like this. We fall out of love again when we think that our partner has changed. Our partner has not really changed; instead, we have learned to see him or her as he or she truly is.

obsession

In psychiatric illness, men can become obsessed with someone who appears to be their perfect partner, even someone they do not know. Young men, in particular, may kill themselves in despair if it becomes clear that a woman on whom they have projected their Anima does not want them. They feel they have lost part of themselves. Media personalities such as Diana, Princess of Wales, movie stars such as Jodie Foster, and many ordinary women have suffered from stalkers who have convinced themselves that their victim is in love with them. This obsession can reach such dangerous heights that the obsessed man thinks that he must possess his love object by kidnapping, breaking in on, or even killing her so that no other man can have her and she can be forever his.

Both Diana, Princess of Wales, and Jodie Foster suffered from stalkers who were obsessed by them.

anima and women

Carl Jung contributed greatly to our understanding of man's image of woman, but full insight into women's psyches has to come from women. Here Toni Wolff had an influence on Jung's ideas. She saw women as falling into four types that relate to the four functions: sensation, feeling, thinking, and intuition.

wife and mother

The wife and mother is the sensible homemaker who provides the secure sanctuary from which her husband and children can venture forth to make their way in the world. Here, of course, we see Emma Jung's early role. The homemaker is queen of her own female domain – her role is separate but equal to her husband. Parenting and homemaking are of equal worth to paid employment, and she is fulfilled in the role of traditional womanhood. The wife and mother is fertile on the earthly plane. In Greek mythology, she is epitomized by the goddess Hera, the queen of the gods and wife of Zeus.

The role of wife and mother is a vital one, as this woman provides security for both her husband and children.

The famous painting by Boticelli, *Venus*, depicts Aphrodite, who was the Greek hetaira figure – a sexual woman who took lovers rather than a husband.

hetaira

The *hetaira's* function is feeling. Hetairas in ancient Greek society were educated women who took men as lovers and friends rather than husbands. In Japanese society, the geisha's role is similar. Toni saw herself as part-hetaira. She had ideas in her own right, but her main goal in life was to support Jung's work. In Greek mythology, the goddess Aphrodite is a hetaira figure. In ancient myth, Aphrodite is born from the foaming waves and is carried to shore naked on a great shell. This is the image found in the beautiful Italian Renaissance painting, the Boticelli *Venus*. She is the epitome of beauty. Aphrodite's nakedness indicates her sexuality, and the waves are symbolic of the waters of the unconscious.

amazon

The Amazon is an independent career woman with her own mission and destiny. Her function is thinking. In Greek mythology, she is represented by

The amazonian career woman is independent and in charge of her life.

two goddesses. Artemis is the huntress goddess who is known in Roman mythology as Diana. Men cross her at their peril. Another independent goddess is Athena, who was the patron goddess of Athens. She was a goddess of intellectual wisdom, but also of war. She is born not of a goddess' womb, but springs fully armed from the side of her father Zeus. Amazon women today might be either successful business or professional women or politicians who compete with men on equal terms. Jung had many "Amazon" women among the first analysts. Women such as Esther Harding were major influences in bringing Jungian analysis to the United States. And in later life, Emma Jung also developed as an analyst in her own right.

medium

Woman as Medium is the intuitive muse who is the voice of creative inspiration. Toni Wolff actually saw herself as part-Medium. In Greek mythology, the goddess Persephone represents

The mysterious, intuitive goddess Persephone from the Underworld is a female medium.

the mysterious otherworld of intuition and spiritual vision. Persephone is stolen away from her mother by the Lord of the Underworld, the god Hades. She is forced to live partly in the Underworld, the mysterious realm of the dead; returning each spring and summer to spend part of the year on the surface of the earth. Persephone is a mediator who brings knowledge from the underworld of the unconscious to the upper realm of conscious awareness. In touch with the collective unconscious, she acts as a priestess to reveal the mysteries of soul and spirit.

a leading female jungian analyst

Dr. Esther Harding was an energetic and pioneering English doctor from a rural area in Shropshire on the Welsh/English border. Esther Harding first met Jung when she was invited to attend a two-week seminar on dream analysis Jung gave at Sennen Cove in Cornwall in 1920. By then, Jung was lecturing in English. Esther was inspired by Jung's ideas and treatment method and in 1923 she helped organize another seminar in Cornwall. She studied with Jung in Zürich and emigrated to the United States where she set up a practice in New York. She later founded the Jung Institute, also in New York.

For many years, Esther returned annually to train with Jung. Esther is famous for her book *Women's Mysteries: Ancient and Modern*, which is about matriarchal Goddess religion. This book had a major impact on women's spirituality and she became a leading figure in Jungian circles in the United States. She endowed the New York Institute with one million dollars on her death in 1971 at the age of eighty-three.

the divine feminine

Jung believed that Christianity's vision of the Divine as a Trinity of Father, Son, and Holy Spirit was flawed because it suppressed the feminine. The balance could be restored if the Divine was no longer seen as solely male; if the Divine also contained the Goddess.

mary

For Jung, Catholicism was superior to the Protestant tradition in that it recognized the Mother of God, if not the Mother Goddess. Jung believed that visions of the Virgin Mary, such as at Lourdes and Fatima, represented a deep-seated need for Goddess as well as God. He was excited by Pope Pius XII's proclamation in 1950 of the doctrine of the Assumption of the Blessed Virgin Mary. This meant that Mary had been taken both body and soul into Heaven. Jung saw it as the most important Christian religious event since the Reformation. Mary had been recognized as having a special superhuman status. She was not yet Divine, but she was the next best thing.

goddess

Jung believed that the images through which we worship the Divine have important psychological impact. An all-male deity can be damaging because this ignores the importance of the feminine. For women, there is the added problem that it does not create a role model to which they can aspire. Mary is limited as a role model for modern women because she is essentially passive. Mary is Mother but also Virgin, and her holiness is derived from submission to a male God. Women today seek to be more in control of their own lives and to integrate sensuality and sexuality as positive life-enhancing experiences. They need a more dynamic model of the Divine feminine.

Jung believed that Mary was an important part of Christianity and represented the need for a female deity.

emma and the divine feminine

Emma Jung wrote that when we reject the Divine feminine we reject Nature and seek to dominate it with masculine intellect and technology. In the world in which we live today, we need urgently to find an accommodation with Nature and a reconciliation with the Divine feminine before the planet that supports us is destroyed.

"When the Anima is recognized and integrated a change of attitude occurs toward the feminine generally. This new evaluation of the feminine principle brings with it a due reverence for nature, too; whereas the intellectual viewpoint dominant in an era of science and technology leads to utilizing and even exploiting nature, rather than honoring her. Fortunately, signs can be observed today pointing in the latter direction. Most important and significant of these is probably the new dogma of the Assumptio Mariae and her proclamation as mistress of creation. In our time, when such threatening forces of cleavage are at work, splitting peoples, individuals, and atoms, it is doubly necessary that those which unite and hold together should become effective; for life is founded on the harmonious interplay of masculine and feminine forces, within the individual human being as well as without. Bringing these opposites into union is one of the most important tasks of present-day psychotherapy." [1]

goddess and god

In Christianity today we see a much greater influence of the feminine. In many denominations, women are becoming pastors and priests. In the Catholic Church today, the Pope is being petitioned to elevate Mary's status further than the 1950 decree and to make her Co-Redemptrix with Christ. The Christian Creation Spirituality movement seeks to sanctify our mother, the Earth. Others are looking outside Christianity and reviving ancient pagan traditions, such as pre-Christian Celtic spirituality, which worshiped Goddess as well as God.

the new eon

Jung believed that Christianity had not yet fully evolved. He was interested in the Book of Revelations and believed that after a phase of destruction on Earth, religious symbols would change. Instead of the male-dominated Trinity of Father, Son, and Holy Spirit, we would worship the Father, the Mother, and the Sun Child, the Child of Promise. This would herald a new era for humankind as masculine destructiveness would be brought into harmony by restoring its balance with the feminine.

Untitled painting by Robert Natkin. Jung felt Christianity had not fully developed but could evolve into a religion that balanced male and female.

[1] Emma Jung. *Animus and Anima: Two Essays* (Spring Publications, 1957), 87.

meeting the divine feminine

This is an active imagination exercise to see what role the divine feminine might play in your life. The exercise takes up to an hour. You will need to be alone in a quiet room. If it is daytime, shut out any bright light. At night, have only soft unobtrusive lighting or candlelight. You will need some plain paper and a pen to write with and some colored pens or pencils to draw with. You could write or type the exercise out in large handwriting so you can see it by dim lighting. Alternatively you could read it onto a cassette so you can play it back to yourself. If you read it onto a cassette, leave gaps for visualization between each instruction.

Start the exercise by gathering paper and pens together – you will use these to draw the experiences you have while meeting with the divine feminine.

finding the divine feminine

1	Close your eyes and take a few moments to relax before beginning.
2	It is night. You find yourself in a grassy place beneath a starlit sky. A full moon bathes you in radiant moonlight.
3	Before you is a path that leads into a forest. Follow the path through the forest until you come to a clearing. When you reach the edge of the clearing, wait.
4	A figure appears from out of the trees and enters the clearing. She is female and represents the feminine aspect of the Divine. You hear her voice speaking softly.

She is calling you to her.

5   You cross the clearing and go to her. You hear her asking, "What do you seek? How can I help you? How can I heal you?" Take five minutes to talk with her to find out how she can help or heal you.

6   You may wish to ask yourself some questions: What are your feelings about the divine feminine in your own life? What part can she play? Take five minutes for this.

7   When you have finished, bid farewell to the Goddess. She may have a gift for you.

Or perhaps you have a gift for her? Take a few minutes for this.

8   It is time to leave the clearing. Go back along the path by which you came. Night is fading. The stars disappear. The sky is growing lighter and turns to blue. You emerge from the forest and return to your grassy place beneath the blue sky of a fresh spring morning.

9   In your own time, find yourself back in your room. Take a little time to return if you need it. Curl up in the fetal position if you wish.

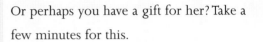

During your journey to meet the divine feminine you will follow a path and enter a forest, where a female figure is waiting for you.

Make notes on your experiences. Write down any thoughts that come to you. Perhaps draw or paint what you have seen. Here are some questions to help you: What was the pathway like which took you to the Goddess? Was it easy or hard? How did the Goddess appear to you: old or young, beauty or crone, or maybe all or none of these? What do you seek from the Goddess? How can she heal you? How can she help you? What part can she play in your life? Did she give you a gift? Or did you give a gift to her?

myths for men

Throughout World War I, Jung was coming to terms with his inner world and with the nature of his Anima. From 1919, when he was forty-three, his life began to open up. He traveled more widely outside Europe and found new insights into his masculinity.

People have always used long journeys for personal and spiritual exploration. By combating difficult conditions and meeting people of other cultures, we stretch our limits and horizons. Although Jung enjoyed women's company, during his travels with male friends outside the West he encountered technologically less advanced societies where the male role was that of warrior, hunter, and leader. As an officer, he was comfortable in these environments.

In 1920, a Swiss friend, Hermann Sigg, invited Jung to accompany him on a business trip to North Africa. North Africa has known many civilizations — Carthaginian, Roman, Christian, Muslim — and many wars. In a land steeped in history, the memories of the past leak into the present.

Jung was entranced by the deep blue Mediterranean sea, the white sands, the dazzling whitewashed houses, and the overwhelming sense of antiquity. In the Tunisian city of Sousse, Jung parted company with Sigg. He was thrilled to be alone among non-Europeans. He was used to strictly timetabled and orderly Switzerland, and North Africa had a more fluid sense of time. A 10:00 meeting could mean 10, or 12 noon, or 2 P.M. Jung loved the attitude of "inshallah" — that things would happen, if it was God's will. He sat in coffee houses where Tunisian men in robes sat for hours, sipping tiny cups of sweet black coffee and fingering their worry beads.

Jung hired mules and rode into the Sahara Desert to the town of Nefta on the Tunisian-Algerian border. Here were people whose lifestyle had changed little over the centuries. At night, the land was plunged into blackness as the sun set. Then, one by one, the stars became visible, sparkling like huge jewels against the indigo sky. With the rising of the white orb of the desert moon, the landscape was bathed in ghostly white. At sunrise and sunset, the muezzin's call to prayers drifted across the rooftops and down into Africa; raising the hairs on the back of the neck with its power.

The Soul's Journey by Rassouli. Exploring both his spirituality and his masculinity was important to Jung while he was in Africa.

africa's
call

Standing at the edge of the Sahara, Jung felt the power of Africa's mystery. An urge to travel onward and downward into Africa's deep heart remained with him and, five years later in 1925, Jung arranged cover for his practice and returned – this time to British-governed Africa.

Jung planned to travel to Kenya, Uganda, Sudan, and Egypt. He needed official backing and so applied to the British government. They acquiesced and gave his party the impressive title of "Bugishu Psychological Expedition." In October 1925, he sailed by steamer for the Kenyan port of Mombasa with an English colleague, Peter Baynes, and an American former patient, George Beckwith (many of Jung's former patients became his friends).

Jung loved to talk to people of different races. In North Africa, his communication was held back by not knowing Arabic. At fifty, learning a new language was difficult, but Jung was determined and managed to learn rudimentary Swahili. After acclimatizing in Mombasa, his party set off for the Kenyan capital of Nairobi, and then went on to the Ugandan border and Mount Elgon, whose streams and rivers feed the Nile. The party had now swelled in numbers and comprised four members. On the boat from England they had met an adventurous young English woman, Miss Ruth Bailey. Much to the horror of her relatives, she decided to join the expedition against their wishes. However, Ruth Bailey was a practical woman who had been a nurse in World War I, and her skills became invaluable when George Beckwith developed malaria.

god's country

Visiting Africa was one of the highlights of Jung's life. For him it was a more enriching experience than just meeting new peoples and learning about a different culture. He was told that this is not "man's country" but "God's country." Jung was inclined to agree. In Africa, he found a sense of divine peace. He was beyond the reach of telephone, letters, patients, and visitors, and this gave him a new freedom that he enjoyed immensely.

Jung enjoyed mixing with people from different races, and his journey to Africa gave him that opportunity.

Through an interpreter, Jung was able to converse with people who had never seen a European before.

asked them about everything he wanted to learn from them — their dreams, thoughts, visions, religious beliefs, and anything he could about their inner life. He was seeking to understand the common humanity that transcended race, culture, and creed. In turn, he found that the Africans had a gift for empathy. He was surprised and pleased to find that they were equally adept as psychologists in their own way.

shaman dreams
no more

In one village, Jung was introduced to a splendidly dressed Masai shaman. Jung asked him if he ever dreamed. Tears came to the old man's eyes as he explained that, yes, once shamans had dreamed. They knew when sickness and war would come, when it would rain, and where the cattle herds should graze. Now the British had come who knew everything. The shamans' dreams were no longer needed. Jung realized the tragedy of colonialization — that it could steal a people's dreams. Jung sensed that soon the people would awaken to their own power and the struggle for independence would begin.

An African shaman uses his traditional witchcraft to heal a member of his tribe.

To reach the 14,000-foot Mount Elgon, the party trekked through rough terrain. Each night lions, leopards, hyenas, and snakes prowled around their tents. Dry savanna turned to lush monkey-chattering jungle. The beauty of Africa and its teeming wildlife was breathtaking. At Mount Elgon, beyond the reach of the colonial government, they entered villages that had seen no Europeans before. Jung wanted to meet and talk with as many of the local people as possible. With the aid of his dictionary and interpreters, Jung eagerly

worship at sunrise

At Mount Elgon, the source of the Nile, people venerated the sunrise, even as the ancient Egyptians had done millennia before. Jung understood that for these Africans, it was not that the sun was God, but that the moment each morning in which the sun was reborn was Divine.

Jung found himself drawn to watch the sun rise every day and to see the first ray of light shoot out like out an arrow to banish the darkness of night. The eastern horizon turned to white and the landscape to crystal flame. Jung felt as if he was inside a temple at the most sacred hour of the day. The baboons sat on a ridge, hands raised, watching in silent stillness.

From Mount Elgon, Jung's party headed by foot, truck, rail, and paddle steamer northward toward Egypt. In Sudan, a chief invited them to witness a male dance. It was a war dance. The party's guides and guards made a discreet and hasty exit, leaving the four Europeans to face the tribesmen alone. By the light of red flickering flames of an enormous fire, spear-bearing warriors bore down; stopping just before their spear tips reached them. The same tribe had killed two white people recently, and it seemed Miss

Many tribes have dances that seem bizarre or even frightening to onlookers but hold particular significance for the participants.

Bailey's relatives' worries were right. The night wore on. The dance grew wilder. The dancers seemed possessed. Things were getting seriously out of control. Jung decided the best policy was to look totally fearless. Seizing a rhinoceros whip, he cracked it against the ground, and he and Peter Baynes leaped in to join the dancers. By distributing gifts and keeping his head, Jung faced it out. The chief decided that he had had enough fun with the white travelers. Far into the night, he let them sleep.

Jung, Bailey, Baynes, and Beckwith sailed the Nile to Egypt so Jung could learn more about Egyptian culture.

With his three "Bs" — Bailey, Baynes, and Beckwith — Jung then sailed down the Nile into Egypt. He wanted to understand ancient Egypt by approaching it from the African culture that was its roots. Traveling twenty-five miles north of the Sudanese-Egyptian border, they first saw the cultural link. They visited the 3,000-year- old temple of the Sun God, Ra, at Abu Simbel. Constructed by Rameses II, Egypt's greatest pharaoh, to mark his thirtieth year of reign, the temple is fronted by four enormous statues of Rameses. Above him, twenty-two baboon statues sit poised on the roof line, their hands raised in prayer to the rising sun, just as their live counterparts in Africa do still.

At Luxor, they crossed to the right bank of the Nile and rode camels to the 3,000-year-old tombs of the Egyptian pharaohs at the Valley of the Kings. They also went to an ancient Christian Coptic monastery. But

The four statues of Rameses in Abu Simbel at the temple of the Sun God that Jung and his companions visited during their journey can be seen in the background.

here there was a small problem for the group; the monastery did not admit women. Not to be held back by rules, Jung immediately decided to dress Ruth Bailey as a man and smuggled her in.

farewell to africa

Impressive though Egyptian culture was, it was in deep Africa that Jung came closer to understanding himself as a man. He had spent six months away, and to leave Africa was a terrible wrench for him. Jung sensed he would not return, which made it even harder. He would never again see the sun reborn in glory each morning out of Africa's dark night.

new mexico

In 1924, Jung spent Christmas in New York before traveling by train to Chicago, a journey of eighteen hours, and then onward to Arizona. He arrived at the Grand Canyon for New Year's Day, 1925.

After a day's sightseeing, the party drove to Taos in New Mexico. By now, Jung was also accompanied by Edith Rockefeller's son, Fowler McCormick. In New Mexico, Professor de Angulo of the University of California at Berkeley introduced Jung to Ochwiay Biano, or "Mountain Lake," a spokesperson for the council of the Taos Pueblo people. The two men quickly developed a strong bond. Pueblo visitors need a good head for heights. Mountain Lake took Jung up five stories of narrow wooden ladders to the roof of the main Pueblo building. Here they sat together through the course of the day, watching the passage of the sun. Mountain Lake further taught Jung to see

Jung developed a friendship with Ochwiay Biano while in New Mexico and was taken to a Pueblo building like this.

Western culture with new eyes. The Pueblo tribes were bewildered by the ever-restless whites who thought with their heads rather than their hearts. To their perception, the whites were always hungry but never satisfied. To Mountain Lake, they seemed quite crazy. Below Jung and Mountain Lake stretched the plateau of Taos. Behind them splashed a stream. Before them were distant volcanoes and a solitary isolated mountain; above them the golden ball of the Sun Father. Everything around them — sun, mountain, water, plain — was sacred to the people.

As Mountain Lake talked, a vision came to Jung of the Roman legions suppressing the ancient Celts and Germans and of Christianity being enforced by the

New Mexico's past recalled for Jung all the sad examples of one culture's dominance over another throughout history.

sword. Columbus, the Conquistadors, the white missionaries; all imposed their culture and religion on others in total ignorance of what they were destroying. The whites had damaged the pueblo dwellers with liquor, syphilis, and infectious diseases, all the time thinking themselves superior. Mountain Lake was right. It was crazy. This was white male aggression unleashed. It seemed to Jung that the masculine in Western culture had lost its way. What was needed was a male initiatory myth that would show men how to live in harmony with the world around them.

myths for men

Jung's midlife experiences in New Mexico and Africa showed him that men such as Mountain Lake, who were still part of an initiatory tradition, had an understanding of their role in the cosmos that white men lacked. The solution was not for white men to adopt Native American culture, but for each culture to find its own solutions. They were there, if only we had eyes to see. Jung had already sensed the importance of heroic myth when he named part of his own journey of growth the Nekyia from the journey of the Greek hero Odysseus. Ten years later, when he came into contact with living tribal culture, Jung began to see patterns in Native American and African myths and beliefs that matched those in the ancient myths and fairytales of Europe. All conveyed in symbol and image the pattern of psychological growth that he called individuation. Individuation was an inner spiritual journey – the ultimate heroic quest.

Jung could see the similarities between Native American and African tribal myths and the ancient tales of the West. He believed the symbolism embodied within each of them spoke of the inner journey each of us must make before we find our true selves.

role models

Today we have more freedom to choose than ever before. We can choose our occupations and whether to become parents. Our families, village elders, and the state no longer make these decisions for us. The downside is that we lack guidance. To understand the masculine, men and women still need strong role models.

missing fathers

The extended family has disintegrated; the nuclear family has broken down. There are no generations of elders to whom we can turn for wisdom and advice. Fathers are frequently absent or might be abusive. We may have no positive male role models from whom to learn.

Jung himself found it difficult to find positive male role models who could help him. Like any small boy, he looked up to his father, Reverend Paul Jung. In adolescence he realized that his father was in an unhappy marriage and struggling to do his job as a minister, while having crises of faith. It seemed to both the Reverend Jung and to his son that his life was a failure. Jung found a

Father figures are extremely important for all of us since they provide us with positive male role models.

substitute father in Freud, but unfortunately Freud was overdependent on Jung. His letters are full of complaints about Jung's slowness in replying to his correspondence – he seems like a nagging mother.

November 11, 1909
Dear Friend,
It probably isn't nice of you to keep me waiting twenty-five days for an answer – as though the promptness of my last letter had frightened you away. I don't wish to importune you in the event that you yourself don't feel the need of corresponding in shorter intervals. Eitingon is the only one I can talk to here. He is leaving tomorrow.
Dr. Freud

January 2, 1910
Dear Friend,
My New Year's greetings have been postponed by my waiting for your letter. I didn't want our correspondence to get out of kilter again.

May 12, 1911
Dear Friend,
This time I have really missed your letters, even more than the news they contain. I am very glad there was nothing worse behind your silence. Because of the long interruption I don't know what I have already told you and what I haven't. I hope you won't wait quite so long before your next letter.[1]

[1] *Freud/Jung Letters*, 163, 170, 224.

guides from within

In Jung's inner Nekyia journey following his break with Freud, his unconscious provided a solution. A figure named Philemon appeared and he was to become his inner guide, his Merlin, the voice beyond the Ego to guide Jung on his journey. Where male role models are missing, the unconscious can help us. Within us is a gateway to the collective unconscious, a psychic inheritance of accumulated human wisdom. Through dream work and therapeutic processes, we can enlist the help of the archetypal figures who come from the unconscious to help us on our journey. Their wider vision can help us break our Ego boundaries and limiting self-images. They inspire us to greater things, to do more than we possibly imagine we can do.

archetypes

The tale of the heroic quest appears in different guises throughout the world, but each follows a similar pattern. A boy of obscure parentage shows early signs of superhuman strength or powers – perhaps he is really the son of a god, hero, or king. He is selected to go on a quest and must suffer trials and tribulations. He is tested and must prove himself against danger, both natural and supernatural. He struggles with the forces of evil. Companions appear who help him. They may be animals, mysterious women with magical powers, or wise magicians and sages. King Arthur, for instance, was assisted by the Lady of the Lake and by Merlin. With their aid, the hero triumphs. He is rewarded with the greatest prize of all, the hand of a royal princess in marriage. He is crowned King.

The young hero in this myth is the Ego. The powers of darkness are the negativity within us. For a man, the royal princess is his Anima, the creativity of the unconscious that helps us on our quest. The wise helpers of the same sex represent the Self, the sum total of the psyche, whose vision exceeds that of the conscious mind.

King Arthur, accompanied by Merlin, asks the Lady of the Lake for the sword Excalibur. Both magical figures aided the king throughout his life.

modern heroes

Stories that mirror the archetypal heroic quest are popular because they also convey messages about their own hero's journey of individuation. The *Star Wars* trilogy tells a classic tale of Luke Skywalker. His first name comes from *lucis*, which is Latin for "of the light." The name Skywalker links him to the sun.

Star Wars is the story of the battle between good and evil, light and darkness – Luke Skywalker and Darth Vader.

star wars

Luke Skywalker is called upon to fight Darth Vader, the servant of darkness, and in doing so discovers this darkness is part of himself. In some myths, the hero's twin brother is his adversary. For Christ it was Satan who had once been Lucifer the Light-Bearer, throne angel of God. For Luke Skywalker, the adversary is his own father. Once a hero, his father was overcome by the power of darkness. The royal woman who helps

Luke Skywalker and whom he must save is his sister. It is his hero companion Hans Solo who wins her. Hans Solo, too, undertakes a journey of transformation; from selfish loner to one who serves a greater good. Only then is he worthy of his bride.

midlife challenge

The hero's crowning is not the end of his journey. With the crowning begins a new set of challenges. He then comes into his maturity. His responsibilities can be burdensome, but there is also a sense of real satisfaction. In modern life, he becomes the father who is looked up to as well as the valued employee.

Our lives peak at this point, then in midlife we begin to realize our human physical frailty. The body itself begins to weaken. Children grow up and become teenagers and challenge their parents' wisdom. Younger people come into the organization seeking promotion and wanting their bosses' jobs.

Once men and women faced very different initiatory challenges, but now both sexes work outside the home and both take a full role in parenting, so the challenges have grown increasingly similar. For a woman in midlife, her career will actually peak. If she is a mother, her children will have grown up and therefore have less need of her. She must let go and loosen the emotional bonds so they can lead adult lives. She must find new sources of intellectual, emotional, and spiritual fulfillment, which may include the workplace.

letting go

In heroic myth, if the king continues listening to his queen and wise companions, he will rule well and will know when to let go of power. But if he listens to his Ego and conscious mind, his Ego becomes

Both men and women make up today's workforce, and the challenge is to learn to work well with a wide variety of colleagues – whether they are male, female, young, or old. This diversity can promote an exciting new experience and be very rewarding.

inflated, and he succumbs to the sin of pride – he then holds onto power when he really should let go. Like the Emperor in *Star Wars*, he becomes a paranoid tyrant and a force of evil. In traditional cultures, elders have a valuable role as wisdom-keepers and initiators of the young. In Western society, the midlife transition is more difficult as this is no longer the case. It involves letting go of Ego ambitions to seek a deeper wisdom. If the Ego is enticed into holding on to ambitions that have run their course, the unconscious will find an answer. The unconscious is purposeful. It wants us to grow. If we do not know how to let go and move forward, the unconscious will engineer our fall. It will enlist the Shadow to trip us up. The hero who became King must now become Merlin.

animus

In the journey of individuation, we must face the demons, ogres, and darkness of our inner world before we find the hidden treasure of the Self. If we are male, the Anima, our inner feminine will help us. If we are women, the Animus, our inner masculine, will appear in our dreams and creative work as a man of bravery, skill, and wisdom to come to our aid.

types of animus

There are four stages of evolution of the Animus. These relate to the four functions. The most primitive form of Animus is the "he-man," like Tarzan, who is close to the animal realm. His is the wild energy of Pan that is unintegrated with society. He is sensate, aggressive, and sexual. The feeling Animus as knightly lover and adventurer is the second stage. He fills the pages of romantic novels. In Arthurian myth, he is Lancelot who risks all for Guinevere. A more modern equivalent would be Leonardo Di Caprio's role as the hero Jack in the film *Titanic*. He gives his life for his lady. King Arthur is the third stage of the Animus. He is the epitome of law. He functions in the realm of thinking. In modern life, he appears in the guise of politician, judge, and businessman. The most evolved fourth stage of the Animus is the sage, priest, magician, or holy man who mediates intuitively between the spiritual and earthly realms. As a woman's psyche evolves, so too will her Animus.

The image of lover and adventurer has been epitomized by Leonardo di Caprio.

The brave Lancelot risked everything, including his life, for the love of his life, the Lady Guinevere.

women and animus

Jung believed that the male images that appear to women in dreams and visions, and the heroes of fiction, fable, and myth, represent undeveloped qualities that women think of as "masculine." These can be difficult for a woman to integrate into her Persona, or self-image. In the era of Carl and Emma Jung, the social roles of men and women were very different. Some women, like Ruth Bailey, did break free of the bounds of convention, but this was definitely not typical. Women found it difficult to live out their urges for adventure, self-determination, and independence. If we are not allowed to be ourselves, we may live vicariously and have unreal expectations of our male partner who must be big, strong, always competent, and wise. Such relationships are doomed to disappointment. The challenge for women is to claim the qualities of the Animus as their own.

the collective animus

Just as women's role has changed, so too have society's Animus images. Until recently, Hollywood movies showed their male heroes as all-powerful — strong, wise, and always knowing best. Their role was to dominate the woman and to protect her from the outside world. In recent movies, hard-bitten heroes have explored their feeling side, and attractive women have explored their heroic natures. Arnold Schwarzenegger played *Kindergarten Cop* and Sigourney Weaver battled in *Alien*. By internalizing in ourselves qualities traditionally associated with the opposite sex, we do not cease to be male or female. We become caring men and dynamic women. Integrating Animus and Anima lets us use all of ourselves rather than forcing ourselves into a straitjacket of traditional sexual stereotyping.

Arnold Schwarzenegger discarded his "macho" image to explore a more caring role in *Kindergarten Cop.*

The attractive Sigourney Weaver became the physical, battling hero in *Alien.*

relating to the masculine

For both men and women, negative family situations and poor fathering can distort our image of the masculine. This can interfere in our relationships with men and in our relationships with God, the masculine aspect of the Divine. In order to relate to the masculine, we need a positive male image. This is an imaginative exercise to help you get in touch with the dynamic and loving aspect of masculine energy. The exercise will take three days to complete. You will find it helpful to draw the Sun Temple. You will need some plain paper and some colored pens or pencils.

days one and two: the sun temple

1   On the first day, draw the Sun Temple. Spend twenty minutes over the first two days practicing visualizing the Temple.

2   The Temple is a square room with golden-yellow walls.

3   Opposite the door is an enormous stained glass window. Its colors are yellow, gold, rose, red, and orange. Sunlight is streaming through, making patterns of colored light on the floor. You may see a picture in the stained glass, or a pattern.

4   In the center of the room is a square altar covered with a gold cloth. On the altar are two candlesticks with lighted yellow candles. Between the candlesticks is a golden vase containing six bright yellow flowers. In front of the vase of flowers is an incense burner. Sweet-smelling incense smoke rises into the temple.

5   Behind the altar and in front of the stained glass window is a high-backed wooden chair.

6   Inside the Temple, it is as warm as a summer's day.

7   Look at your drawing of the Sun Temple. Make a mental image of the Temple. Visualize it a stage at a time: the room, then the altar, the objects on the altar, and the chair. Now try and hold a complete image of the Temple in your mind.

Once you have drawn the Temple, close your eyes and try to visualize it.

day three: sun god

The next stage is a visualization of the solar god. In Irish mythology, he is Lugh. To the Norse, he is Baldur the Beautiful. He is also known as Ra, Helios, and Apollo. Alternatively, you could visualize Christ the Risen King if you wish. You will need a piece of plain paper to draw on, some colored pens or paints, and a quiet space to do this part of the exercise.

1   Visualize the Sun Temple, as before.

2   The Temple is warm and sweet-smelling. You feel a great sense of peace and relaxation. Bright sunlight streams through the stained glass window.

3   The light through the window becomes brighter and brighter. The light begins to form a column of golden light on the floor behind the altar in front of the high-backed chair.

4   The golden light begins to take the shape of a tall man with long flowing hair. You sense a presence of great power, gentleness, and love.

5   The figure becomes solid, three-dimensional. The Sun God has appeared. Commune with him for a while. Ask him to tell you what role the masculine should play in your life. He may have a gift to give you or you give a gift to him.

6   When you feel the time is right, bid him farewell and let his presence fade.

7   Afterwards, make some notes. Describe the Sun God's appearance, your feelings and sensations, and any message or gift he had for you. You could draw or paint an image of the Sun God.

This is an exercise that you can repeat on any occasion when you feel you need dynamic solar energy in your life. You may find it helpful on the day before a job interview, when you have major tasks at work, or on other occasions when you need to assert yourself or take the lead or initiative. The sun's energy is healing, and you may therefore find the exercise particularly helpful if you are recovering from illness. Instead of questioning the Sun God on these occasions, ask him to help you with your task.

dark side of the psyche

> Jung had worked with psychiatric patients, with people who had committed crimes, and with those that were racked with guilt about past misdeeds. He realized that within all of us, no matter who we are, there are negative impulses that lead us to actions that seem totally outside our normal personalities. Even in childhood, Jung felt the darker sides of the individual human psyche.

Jung remembered his mother saying to him that he had always been a good boy. The idea was strange to him. As an introspective spiritual child and adolescent, Jung looked into himself more deeply than others of his age. He acknowledged his own negative impulses and more shameful thoughts.

As a young child, it seemed to Jung that he had recognized a hidden side to the human psyche in himself and others that no one was willing to discuss. Even in his own home, where there were theological discussions, no one talked about the gift of grace that could come when people were willing to confess to themselves the negativity that lay behind their conventional masks. Jung began to feel that he knew too much about people. He had seen behind the Persona to what lay beneath, but this knowledge was too great for a child. Like many children who are old beyond their years, he felt inwardly lonely. His ideas were beyond the understanding of his school friends, but adults would not discuss the deep complexities of human nature with a child. It is no wonder that when he came to study psychiatry, Jung realized that at last he was encountering a body of knowledge that could provide the answers he sought.

Psychiatry was for Jung the gateway that he had been looking for to help him understand the human psyche. However, while working in the Burghölzi Clinic in 1900, he still had some doubts about the methods of psychiatry. It was a medical discipline so, as doctors, psychiatrists were trained to observe their patients' outer behavior, to list their symptoms, and to make a diagnosis and classify them. This meant that the deeper aspects of patients' problems might never be touched upon at all. Freud's work, therefore, became of the utmost importance to Jung because Freud's methods for interpreting dreams offered him the means to understand the problems that each of his patients had repressed.

The Contact by Rassouli. From a very early age, Jung knew he had the ability to look deep into the human psyche.

guilt and illness

One of Jung's early patients at the Burghölzi Clinic was a young woman on one of the wards who had been classified as schizophrenic. Her prognosis was poor, and it seemed she would be permanently hospitalized. Jung was convinced that she was not schizophrenic, but that she was suffering from deep depression.

Jung began to reinvestigate the young woman's case, talking to her about her dreams and also trying out the word association test. Jung found that she reacted strongly to certain words, and he became certain that she saw herself as a murderess. Bit by bit, he managed to piece together her story. She had been in love with a young man who was the son of a wealthy industrialist and one of the most eligible young men of the neighborhood. She thought he had no interest in her, so she married someone else. Five years and two children later, a friend confided that the industrialist's son had been interested in her. He had been deeply shocked when she married another man. Through miscommunication, the young woman had missed marrying the love of her life.

Her unconscious desires took over, and resentment and anger at her mistaken marriage began to eat at her. She wanted to destroy the marriage and all it had brought. The water supply where she lived was contaminated and could not be used for drinking, although it was used for washing. One day she was bathing her four-year-old daughter when she saw the little girl sucking at her sponge. The mother stared with a strange fascination and did nothing. A few weeks later, the little girl developed typhoid fever and

died. Wracked with guilt and despair, the woman fell into a severe depression. She developed suicidal tendencies and had to be hospitalized. Although Jung had managed to put together the jigsaw, his patient had never acknowledged to herself what she had done. The burden was too great, and she had fled from it into madness.

He told her everything that he had discovered and enabled her to confront the reality of what had happened for the first time. She shouldered the burden of the knowledge of her guilt and began to recover. Two weeks later, she had recovered enough to be discharged. Jung believed her months in the mental hospital had been punishment enough and no further action should be taken against her. She reentered her life endeavoring to become a good wife and mother to her remaining child.

Untitled painting by Robert Natkin. By using the word association test and analyzing dreams, Jung was able to fit together the pieces of his patient's unconscious life.

Jung was faced with an enormous dilemma. He was still young and inexperienced and did not think he could tell his superiors at the Burghölzi what he had discovered. They would advise forgetting it, either because it would exacerbate the young woman's illness or, if she admitted it to them all, it could leave them in a difficult legal position. Jung decided to act.

the shadow of war

Jung was aware not only of the Shadow in individuals. He was also aware of the darker side of the collective psyche. When Jung returned from Africa in 1926, there were already signs of the Nazi Shadow that was to overwhelm Europe. It seemed to him that there was something in the German psyche in particular at the time that was extremely dangerous.

Jung could see that Nazism held a dangerous fascination which drew many German people to it.

swept up in the tide

Jung's paternal grandfather was German, and German was his first language. Although C. G. Jung considered himself first and foremost a Swiss, he was a Swiss German. In recognizing dark forces within the German psyche, he also felt he was recognizing them within himself.

As a therapist, Jung was against any mass movement that could make people forget their own individual ethics and morals. As a Swiss German, he could understand the compelling fascination that Hitler had for Germans. Rational, educated German friends experienced a tide of emotion that had washed all their reason away. Nowadays, this can be

When Nazis organized attacks against Jews, Jung was concerned for Freud's safety, since Freud was still in Vienna.

hard to understand, but initially Nazism seemed to offer the German nation hope of a brighter future. Germany in the 1920s was suffering an economic disaster with millions of people unemployed. Hitler's dictatorship worked what seemed an economic miracle, putting people back into jobs. Few people believed he would take his policies to their extreme.

Soon Nazi intentions became clear. In 1938, Austria was annexed into their empire. Jung's first concern was for Freud who was still in Vienna. It was possible for some Jews to escape, provided they could pay the Nazis vast sums of money. Jung raised from his own funds and that of others what was then a vast sum of money – $10,000. A colleague's son was sent quickly to Vienna with the cash hidden in a money belt. The trip proved useless. Freud refused to accept help from those he saw as his enemies. Fortunately others intervened, and Freud was able to leave Vienna for the relatively safe London.

World War II broke out in September 1939. In May 1940, the French Vichy government signed a peace agreement with the Nazis. This partitioned France into two zones – a nominally free zone and a German-occupied zone. Hitler could now expand in other directions. Little Switzerland seemed a likely candidate. Jung's opinions about Nazism were now clear, and his name was on a Nazi blacklist. He was warned by the Swiss authorities that he should leave Zürich and flee to the mountains. Fortunately for Jung and his fellow Swiss, the invasion threat passed. Circumstances had forced Hitler to turn his attentions elsewhere.

confronting the shadow

Jung's early fascination with Nazism troubled his conscience greatly. In 1945, he wrote an article "After the Catastrophe" exploring his guilt feelings and what it is to be aware of a sense of one's own evil.

"I had not realized how much I myself was affected. There are others I am sure who will share this feeling with me. This inner identity of participation mystique with the events in Germany has caused me to experience afresh how painfully wide is the concept of collective guilt. So when I approach this problem it is certainly not with any feelings of cold-blooded superiority, but rather with an avowed sense of inferiority."[1]

Jung had never been involved in any Nazi activities, and yet he was deeply troubled that he had been drawn to its early promises.

Jung believed that we must be willing to confront our own guilt and found an opportunity to do just that himself in 1946. Jung arranged a meeting in Zürich between himself and the famous Rabbi Leo Baeck who had been imprisoned in the Theresienstadt concentration camp. Leo Baeck reproached Jung for his attitudes in the 1930s, and Jung acknowledged that he had been wrong. His hopes that something positive might emerge from the Nazi regime had been misguided. Jung's admission brought about a reconciliation between these two famous men and they parted friends. As Jung himself had written of analysis: the first stage is confession.

Leo Baeck (left) was the president of the Jewish Counsel for Germany, and Jung sought him out in order to confront his own feelings of guilt.

[1] C. G. Jung, "After the Catastrophe" (1945) in *The Collected Works of C. G. Jung,* vol. 10, *Civilization in Transition.* 2d ed. (Routledge & Kegan Paul, 1996), para. 402.

what is the shadow?

Our Shadow is made up of impulses we see as undesirable and have tried to repress. It also includes qualities that are undeveloped but could become positive if we learn how to use them well. The fourth and least developed of our personality functions is part of our Shadow.

seeking approval

We are all aware of having an image to maintain. We have a Persona, a cleaned-up version of ourselves that we present to the world. Personas help facilitate social interaction. We cover our negative characteristics under a veneer of polite decorum. If we did not, society would not function very well. The Shadow is made up of all those unpleasant bits of ourselves that we hide beneath a social veneer. Many of these are biological urges that are part of our primitive human beginnings, such as hate, jealousy, and aggression. They are closely related to impulses we express as toddlers. We learn quickly that some of these are frowned upon by our families and our kindergarten friends. We learn guilt and shame, and we repress our negative impulses below the surface of consciousness. We do this to win the approval of others. We also like to fool ourselves that we are the people we would like to be. This self-deception is dangerous. It leads us to attribute the most worthy of motives to our actions, when the opposite may be true.

self-awareness

Most of us are aware that we have negative qualities, although there are some people who think they are perfect. Mercifully, these people are rare. But actually, why do we instinctively dislike people who like themselves too much? Is it because we sense that behind the mask is a layer of negativity that the individual does not want to acknowledge, but that we know is there just as it is in us? People who admit their own imperfections are much easier to like than those who do not.

Underneath our socially acceptable veneer, our shadow personality contains our negative aspects that we try to suppress.

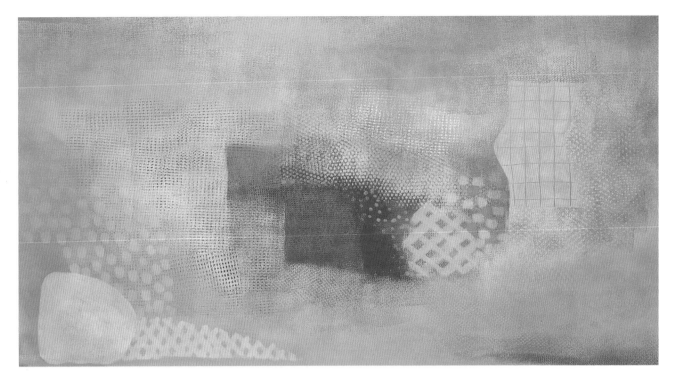

Untitled painting by Robert Natkin. All of us have light and darkness in our lives – our primitive, biological urges such as jealousy and hate lurk in the shadows.

Facing up to our Shadow, rather than hiding it even from ourselves, is an important part of self-awareness.

meeting our shadow

The Shadow is often at work when we meet someone of the same sex who, for some unknown reason, we instantly dislike. Instinctively, we decide that we can't stand that woman, or say that he's just not our type of guy. Like a cat meeting a dog, the hairs bristle on the back of our necks. There could be good reasons for not liking these people – maybe they are not nice people. If, however, you meet someone whom all your friends like and you cannot stand, maybe it is because you recognize something in that person that you do not like in yourself, the result being that something jars in you every time you see them. This can be a hard concept to accept, but think about it. The next time you meet someone and find you cannot stand them after about ten seconds, think about projection again.

self-image

We try to live up to our own self-image. This is normal. The problem is that to help us maintain our self-image; the Shadow manipulates us into some very convoluted thinking. It is easy to invent of all sorts of reasons as to why it is justifiable to harm others.

self-deception

This is the syndrome of the self-deceived mother whose jealousy of her pretty daughter makes her buy the girl unattractive clothes so that "she does not get too full of herself." It is the father who sends his artistic son to military college "because it will be good to toughen him up." Really he is afraid that his friends at work will think his son is effeminate and, by extension, if his son is, perhaps he is too.

projection

We not only disguise our own motives; we also project them onto others. Repressed qualities and energy must go somewhere. When we refuse to see our worst faults in ourselves, then we see them in others. Have you ever heard someone ranting about how intolerant other people are? How often have you met the stingiest of people who talk constantly about how stingy other people are; or the rampant egoist who is convinced everyone else is egotistical?

Projection can lead to extreme behavior; especially when we delude ourselves that we are doing good. The serial killer projects his own inner evil onto others. He believes that by killing women, prostitutes, homosexuals, or whomever, he is cleansing society of

evil. Whole social groups can be infected with these delusions. The Inquisition tortured heretics because misguided clerics thought they were saving the souls of their victims. Nazis deluded themselves that they were "cleansing the race." The communist Pol Pot regime in Cambodia killed two million people to rid their country of the scourge of "bourgeois elements."

the shadow in dreams

We may become aware of our Shadow in dreams. Many people dream of being chased by something or someone large and frightening. It may be an animal, an armed man, an alien, or some more abstract evil force. Often the pursuer represents aspects of ourselves – the Shadow – that we are unwilling to face. We can free ourselves from such dreams. Every evening before you go to sleep, tell yourself that if you are chased you will turn around and confront whatever is chasing you. This is unlikely to work the first time you try, and maybe the next, but keep telling yourself that this is what you will do. Sooner or later you will have a lucid dream. A lucid dream is one in which you consciously realize that you are dreaming. You will become aware that you are being chased, and you will discover that you can turn around and face what is behind. Whatever it is will then become less frightening and will shrink as a result. When our Shadows are less frightening to us, then we can begin to own them. As long as we stay afraid of what is within, we will hide from it.

By projecting their own evil onto innocent victims,
some people can delude themselves into thinking that
their inappropriate behavior is justified.

splinter personality

Jung often talked about the Shadow as a "splinter personality." It seems to have a life of its own. We experience the Shadow when we find ourselves saying, "I don't know what came over me. I don't know what made me do that."

trickster

We try to repress our negative impulses, but they want to get out. Allowing the Shadow to "escape" might seem the last thing we would want to do, but we cannot deal with it until we are aware of its existence. Paradoxically, the Shadow tries to help us here. Many mythologies have a Trickster who entices us into revealing our negative side. For instance, Brer Rabbit in American folk tradition, Loki in Norse mythology, and the Devil in European folk tales all play this role. The Trickster leads us into all sorts of confused behavior. We tell lies that are obviously untrue. We become involved in extramarital affairs that are bound to be found out. The Shadow insists on showing us who we really are. This is not necessarily bad, though it can be painful at the time. When the Ego becomes inflated, the Shadow allies with the Self to expose us. For instance, in the dream cited earlier, Jung's Shadow helped him shoot down "Siegfried." As Jung wrote, "The dream showed that the attitude embodied by Siegfried, the hero, no longer suited me. Therefore it had to be killed." [1]

transforming the shadow

We do not want our negative qualities exposed, but if we face up to ourselves as we really are, then we can

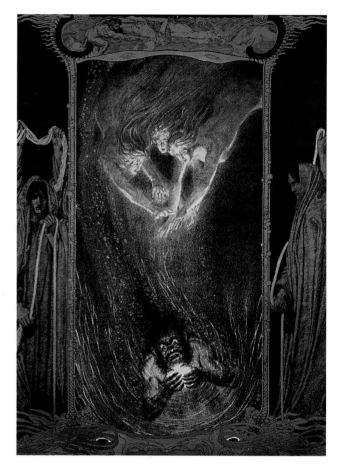

Myths have many examples of characters who entice us into revealing our negative sides.

do something about the things we really don't like. We begin to feel better about ourselves and, in turn, feel better about others. Once we begin to confront the Shadow, we can even discover that many qualities that we have learned to repress can actually be useful if properly channeled. The positive side of anger is energy. Energy can be channeled into doing something constructive about the situation that made us angry. The positive side of jealousy can be the urge to do something to improve the quality of our own

[1] *Memories, Dreams, Reflections*, 180.

lives, rather than being negative about the lives of others. The Shadow can be thought of as an energy blockage. Our negative feelings are suppressed and eat away at us. Instead of finding a useful way of transforming aspects of ourselves or situations that we do not like, we become passive and trapped.

confession

To transform the Shadow, first we must know it exists. Carl Jung often likened the first stage of analysis to the Catholic confessional. During this stage we need to unburden ourselves of our shames, fears, and guilts. Our lives can be transformed by confessing all the negative things that we have been carrying within us, and we will feel released. This cleansing and release is essential if we are to move forward. It is a recognition of the Shadow within. Acknowledging the Shadow is an important piece of spiritual work. It is only by changing ourselves that we can begin to change society. All spiritual systems teach us that the path to self-knowledge is long and hard. We must descend into the dark valley before we can ascend once more into the light. And in that dark, secret, silent place where we can be alone, there we can take the courageous step of facing the Shadow and looking into the mirror of truth.

From the *Hitchcock* series by Robert Natkin. We must all confront the dark areas in our inner selves.

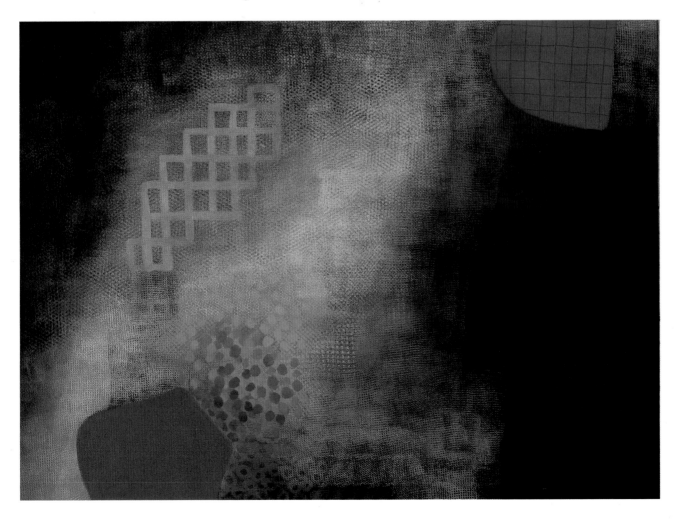

getting to know the shadow

the triangles exercise

This is an exercise to help you know your Shadow. It is the first stage in bringing what is unconscious into consciousness. This does not mean that through this exercise we will recognize all our negative patterns, but it is a good way to start learning to do it.

Do the exercise on two separate days, three days apart. You will need a quiet room, four sheets of plain paper, and a pen. The exercise takes up to one hour per session. A bath or shower beforehand will help you unwind. You might like to light a perfumed candle to help stimulate your unconscious mind, but do carry out the exercise before 6:00 in the evening, because, at night, our negative qualities seem much worse than they are.

first day

1   On a sheet of paper draw a large triangle. In the center write:

"Triangle 1: My negative qualities"

Think about your personality and write down all of your most negative characteristics. These may be things that are "bad," such as envy, deceitfulness, being unwilling to take the blame. They may alternatively be characteristics that are not so much bad as weaknesses – for instance, fears of inadequacy.

With your unconscious mind stimulated, the first step of this exercise is to draw a triangle.

2   On another sheet of paper, draw a second triangle, and write in the center:

"Triangle 2: How my worst enemy sees me"

Think of someone of your own sex who really dislikes you. Write down the negative qualities he or she might say you have. This does not mean, of course, that the person is right. To help, think about things that people have accused you of in the past.

3   On another sheet of paper, draw a third triangle, and write in the center:

"Triangle 3: How I see my worst enemy"
List the negative qualities of the person who really dislikes you.

second day (three days later)

1   Compare your three triangles with one another.
Are there any common characteristics?
If so, these are areas that worry you and you will need to work on. Are there any common points between how a critic might describe you and your description of her or him?
 Think about the qualities that come up on both these two lists.
Are there any occasions when you display these qualities?
What are these occasions?
Are there ways you can change how you behave?

2   Now take a sheet of paper and head it:
"Triangle 4: Triangle of transformation"

3   Look at the negative traits you think you have. How could you transform these into positive qualities? Could your anger become energy; your apathy the ability to relax; your greed a connoisseur's enjoyment of fine food?

4   Select two things from this list that you can work on to change. Do not select more than two since change is best achieved slowly and steadily.

Your greed can be transformed and channeled so that you become a connoisseur rather than a glutton.

Many qualities we see as negative may not seem so to others. Often we get things wrong or exaggerate our faults. If you have someone whom you trust, show them Triangle 1, your negative qualities. Ask if he or she agrees. Maybe qualities you view as very offensive are hardly noticeable to others. A trusted friend or partner may also be able to help you think of ways you can transform your negative qualities.

east meets west

Jung had long been familiar with Eastern spirituality. As a child, his mother read to him tales of Hindu deities and throughout his adult life he studied Hinduism, Buddhism, and Chinese Taoism. In his major work Symbols of Transformation, he wrote extensively about Eastern traditions. Many of his psychological concepts were drawn from the spirituality of the East.

When Jung first met Professor Sigmund Freud, it seemed he had found a teacher or mentor who could help him on his quest to understand the mysteries of the psyche. When the relationship failed, Jung was thrown back on his own resources. In the midst of his 1913–19 Nekyia crisis, inner guides began to appear in his dreams and visions to help him. First of all, the image of the prophet Elijah came to him. With Elijah was a blind Anima figure, a woman called Salome. As Jung's inner integration progressed, so too did his inner teacher. Elijah and Salome disappeared and were replaced by a strange new figure whom Jung called Philemon. Philemon had the horns of a bull, the wings of a kingfisher, and held in his hands four keys. Jung's psyche had produced an image of the four functions held together by a fifth mode of consciousness that transcended them all. Jung sensed that Philemon represented the wisdom of the ancient Greek, Egyptian, and Gnostic mystery traditions. He found that he could hold interior conversations with Philemon where he received wisdom and teaching.

Philemon became Jung's inner teacher, but he puzzled Jung. Who was he? It was not until years later that Jung found anyone who had a similar experience. He was visited by an Indian sage who was a friend of Mahatma Gandhi, the world-renowned leader who helped bring about the liberation of India from British rule with great bravery through his method of peaceful protest. Jung's Indian visitor explained to him the relationship between a guide and "chela" or pupil. Jung asked his visitor if he had a guru. The visitor indicated that indeed he did—an eighth-century Hindu sage and saint named Shankara. He went on to explain that while most people had living guides, some had spirit teachers within. Such was Jung's Philemon.

Symphonic Dance by Rassouli. Jung turned to the East to find sources of inspiration and harmony. The traditions he found influenced his writings.

journey to the east

Over the years, Jung's knowledge of Eastern traditions deepened. In the 1930s he studied yoga and the chakras and began to write extensively about them. Jung's works began to be well known in Indian academic circles. In 1938, he was invited to the twentieth anniversary celebrations of the University of Calcutta. He went on to receive one honorary doctorate at Calcutta and then two more at Allahabad and Varanasi universities. Varanasi, then known as Benares, is one of the holiest cities of Hinduism.

Jung had not visited Asia before, so the invitation gave him the ideal opportunity to make an extended visit to India and Sri Lanka. He took a steamer from Marseilles in southern France across the Mediterranean, down the Suez Canal, and around the Arabian Gulf to the busy Indian port of Bombay, where he began exploring Asia.

The Himalayas duly cast their spell upon Jung, as did viewing the wonder of the sunset with Indian scientists at the Darjeeling Observatory. In India and Sri Lanka, Jung felt more at home in Buddhist than in Hindu temples. He was inspired by Buddha, whom he felt was a spiritual psychologist like himself. The restrained austerity of Buddhism held a great appeal for him. At the stupas of Sanchi, a most impressive

When Jung visited India, he was profoundly affected by the natural surroundings and was inspired by Buddha.

Buddhist site, Jung watched as Japanese pilgrims came in procession striking small gongs and chanting, Om mani padme hum "Hail jewel in the lotus." The jewel in the lotus became, for Jung, an evocative image of the Self. Jung found himself gripped by a powerful insight – the Lord Buddha had understood the dignity and wonder of human consciousness and had sought to awaken it in us all.

from east to west

Jung believed the West overemphasized the rational, intellectual, and scientific side of life. Western culture was for him an extroverted culture that still sought power and control over the earth and her resources. He felt that we have made great technological advances and created complex civilizations, but have ignored our inner life. The West had mapped the material world, but the East had mapped the interior world. Jung was fascinated by Eastern spirituality, but India was a long way from the bare-floored, plain Protestant churches of Jung's youth. For him there was a culture gap. He did not feel he could become a Hindu or Buddhist. He felt himself to be a Westerner in need of a spiritual tradition rooted in the culture of the West. He was sure that the transformation of consciousness offered through Eastern systems must be available in the West. But where?

eastern ceremonies

Simple actions and ceremonies spoke to Jung in a way that complex doctrines and creeds could not. When he was in Sri Lanka, he attended an evening drumming ceremony in the Temple of the Holy Tooth of Buddha at Kandy. Five drummers took up position in the outer hall of the temple, the manapam or Hall of Waiting; one in each corner and one at the center. The central drummer offered his drum in homage before the golden statue of Buddha, and then they began. Jung felt the ancient language of the drum, which speaks not to the mind, but to the belly and solar plexus. Afterward, young men and women poured enormous mounds of jasmine blossom in front of the temple altars and used chants such as the example here. Jung was profoundly moved.

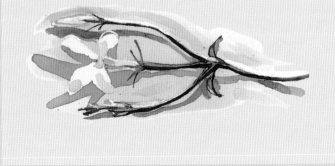

"This life is as transitory as the beauty of these flowers; may my guardian spirit share the merit of this offering with me."[1]

[1] This chant was recalled by Jung in *Memories, Dreams, Reflections*, 314.

a western tradition

At the age of sixty-three, Jung found some aspects of his trip to India difficult. When he had been in Africa, his robust health had helped him avoid sickness. In Calcutta, he succumbed to dysentery and spent ten days in the hospital. One night in his hotel room, just after he had left the hospital, Jung had a significant dream.

Throughout his life, Jung was blessed with vivid dreams. Whenever he had a dilemma, his unconscious would send him an answer. In Calcutta, far away from Christian Europe, he dreamed about the Grail. He was with some friends from Zürich on an unknown island. He felt the island was off the southern coast of England. He was standing in the courtyard of a medieval castle, which he knew to be the Castle of the Grail. The Grail is a mythical chalice said, by some, to be the cup in which Christ blessed the wine that was used for the Last Supper. Others say it is the cup in which the blood of Christ was collected as he hung on the cross. Jung sensed that it was the eve of a feast to celebrate the Grail.

Inside the castle he could see a columned candlelit hall that seemed warm and inviting, but he did not enter. Instead, Jung found himself with his friends outside the castle. Jung realized that this jump outside meant that the Grail was not yet in the castle. It was in an uninhabited house north of the island and someone must fetch it for the celebration. Jung and his friends set off to tramp the barren rocky landscape to bring back the precious relic. They reached a stretch of water as night fell. Jung realized that the island was divided almost in two by a wide inlet from

After his time in the hospital, Jung dreamed of the Grail. During his dream, he realized that he was the lone crusader who must carry it back to the castle.

the sea. It was too far to go around the inlet, and there was no bridge or boat. By now the party was exhausted. One by one, all of his companions fell asleep until only Jung was left awake. There was no option for him. He would have to swim the channel alone to fetch the Grail. Then he woke up.

the grail

The Grail has become a Christian symbol, but long ago it symbolized the Cauldron of Cerridwen, the Welsh Celtic Mother Goddess. In Irish mythology, it was the Cauldron of the Dagda, the Good God, which could never be emptied and in which warriors could be reborn. The miraculous vessel of transformation has obvious associations with the womb that transforms us from egg to human child. It is also associated with the alchemist's spherical vessel in which base matter is turned to spiritual gold. As he sailed home from the East, Jung realized that his vision was taking him not into Eastern spirituality, but back into the esoteric traditions of the West. In the final years of his life, he immersed himself in the study of the ancient Western tradition of alchemy.

The Grail is a mythical symbol of transformation, but it also holds associations with alchemy. Jung became interested in alchemy in his later years.

a spiritual quest

The aim of Jung's analytical psychology evolved from bringing healing to the sick to seeking psychospiritual transformation for the healthy. Healthy people suffer from the issues and problems that face us all: how to live meaningfully and in harmony with our bodies, ourselves, and others in a way that can bring us inner peace.

eastern spirituality

Jung did not find the answers he sought in Protestant Christianity. Protestantism actually seemed to him to offer form and dogma, but held no key to inner transformation. First he looked at the Gnostic texts that had been suppressed by the Christian tradition. It seemed to Jung that the Gnostics were spiritual psychologists who were pursuing the same goals as himself. However, the Gnostics had been branded as heretics and so had never had the opportunity to develop their tradition fully. It was to find similar spiritual insights into the nature of the human psyche that Jung turned to the East.

yoga

Yoga is found in Hinduism, Buddhism, and Taoism, and advanced states of consciousness can be achieved through yoga practice. It involves all the senses and uses bodily postures, gestures, and sound *mantras* (or chants), *yantras* (visual images), sacred patterns including *mandalas* (devotional offerings of flowers and incense), *prana-yama* (breath control), and *dhyana* (concentration). The yoga postures stimulate centers or chakras in the body that are linked to our glandular

Yoga teaching has spread from East to West and it is a good way of relaxing the body. However, it also changes the consciousness, and this is what fascinated Jung.

systems and, as a result, yoga can enhance physical health. It also causes changes in consciousness. Carl Jung used the term "yoga" to mean the whole range of Eastern wisdom represented by Buddhism, Hinduism, and Taoism. He was aware of the physical health benefits of yoga, but this was not his main interest. For Jung, yoga was a specialized system of consciousness change that had a final goal of self-realization. He believed that the pursuit of this goal was the unifying theme throughout the religions and spirituality of the East. He contrasted this with the Western approach of worshipping an external and transcendent God. In the East, the Divine was within.

alchemy

Jung's Grail dream in India led him to reexamine the Western esoteric tradition of alchemy with the insights he had gained from the wisdom of the East. Yoga transforms the body, mind, and spirit: alchemy is ostensibly about changing base metal to gold, but Jung believed the outer operation was simply a metaphor for a more profound inner change. He realized that alchemy was not just an early scientific and technical process. It involved an elaborate cosmology in which the human being, the microcosm, was a reflection of the cosmos, the macrocosm. Since macrocosm and microcosm reflect one another, by engaging in the transformation of matter, the alchemists would at the same time transform their own consciousness. Jung believed that the alchemists were projecting onto matter their own psychic processes. Some were aware of the deeper symbolic meaning, but many were not. However, the preparations involved in alchemical work hint at the spiritual discipline involved. Practitioners had to be in a state of spiritual purity and had to renounce all covetousness. The attitude was to be one of detachment and compassion, and the work accompanied by prayer.

Jung found that many of his patients who were undergoing inner changes on their journey of individuation had dreams that resembled the processes described in alchemy. For him, the stages of alchemy became a sophisticated symbol system that represented the archetypes of the collective unconscious and the different stages of the individuation process.

The physical process involves a series of scientific operations using furnaces of varying temperatures, stills, flasks, and the alchemist's miraculous spherical vessel. As the base metal in their scientific apparatus divided into male and female elements and then reunited again to a new and precious substance that contained both male and female, so too did the alchemists' souls.

Alchemists use a variety of materials and, along with flasks and stills, the spherical vessel is the most used and most important instrument.

transformation

Both alchemy and yoga have as their goals a transformation that is, at the same time, physical and spiritual. This transformation can be equated to the changes in the psyche brought about by Jungian analysis. There are four stages to this process.

nigredo

First there is the stage of purification. In alchemy this is called *nigredo*, or blackness. In Jungian analysis this is confession. We confront the Shadow, acknowledging the negative impulses within us. Initially, this can lead to depression as we realize our own unworthiness and self-deceptions. But, as we learn to accept our own failings, light begins to shine through. In alchemy, the substance produced by the nigredo begins to show white flecks. In therapy, the psyche is being cleansed.

albedo

The substance in the alchemist's miraculous spherical vessel washes clean and then becomes volatile and crystallizes. The substance eventually achieves *albedo*, or whiteness. In yoga, this is the stage of identification and internalization. Instead of worshipping and showing devotion to a deity, the worshiper identifies with the deity. In Jungian analysis we enter the stage of elucidation or explanation. We begin to understand ourselves and to conduct a dialogue with the arche-typal figures within. There is an encounter with the Anima or Animus. None of this is achieved without suffering; but through the purgatorial fire of self discovery, the unconscious becomes illuminated and the albedo, or whiteness, stage is reached.

rubedo

In alchemy the white substance is now heated, and we reach the stage of *rubedo*, or redness. Symbolically, the white substance was often equated with the moon and the heating fire with the warmth of the sun. This might be depicted as a sacred marriage between a white queen and red king. In yoga, the third stage is harmony and equilibrium which, in Jungian analysis, corresponds to the stage of education. We recognize the opposite and conflicting tendencies between

Detail from "Epiphany" by Robert Natkin. The symbolic marriage between white queen and red king is known as the *rubedo* stage in alchemy. In this stage we learn to balance our Ego and Shadow.

lower chakras and the lunar and solar currents within the body harmonize, and inner conflict ceases. As a result, we are energized.

opus magnum

The fourth stage in yoga is unity-merging. Masculine and feminine energies are balanced, and a new consciousness is born. In alchemy, the unification of opposites creates a new being or substance. In the alchemical tests, the outcome is represented variously as the elixir of life that brings longevity; as a winged hermaphrodite representing unity of body, soul, and spirit; or as the Philosopher's Stone that bestows all wisdom. This is the completion of the *Opus Magnum*, or "Great Work". In Jungian analysis, the opposites within are synthesized. We give birth to a new vantage point in consciousness – the transcendent function, the Self, the goal of individuation.

Persona and Anima or Animus, and between Ego and Shadow, and we find ways to accommodate the positive qualities of each. We learn to recognize and use all four functions of the personality – thinking, feeling, sensation, and intuition. From a center of balance and harmony, we find that we are more in control of our inner psyches and, hence, our outer lives. In yoga, the physical body is controlled by postures and breathing techniques that promote physical and psychological well-being. The upper and

The transformation process that yoga and alchemy share as a goal is also what Jungian analysis seeks to achieve.

finding the balance

the cup and sword exercise

Within us are many competing and opposing energies. To move forward on our spiritual path, we must find a point of integration among them. To find that point of integration, we must first learn their balance within us.

This is an exercise to experience two different types of energy that we all possess. Do the exercise without thinking too much about the symbolism. Let your unconscious mind take you on a journey. Afterward, you may want to think more about what the symbols mean for you. The exercise takes up to an hour. You will need to be alone in a quiet, darkened room. You will also need to gather together some large plain paper, a pen to write, and some colored pens or pencils to draw. You could memorize the details, or you could write or type the exercise out in large print so you can see it by dim lighting. Alternatively, you could read the text onto a cassette so you can play it back to yourself. In this case, leave gaps for visualization between each instruction.

the first stage of your journey

1   Relax for a few moments. Imagine yourself in daytime in a green and pleasant meadow at the foot of a mountain. Spend a few minutes orienting yourself to the space and exploring. Notice its sounds and smells as well as its sights.

2   Once you feel fully at one with the place, walk across the meadow toward the mountain. You decide to explore the mountain and begin to follow a path up the lower slopes. Allow yourself 3–5 minutes to explore the lower slopes. While you are doing this you will find either a sword or a cup.

3   When you find either the cup or sword, pick it up. You may want to say something or make some gesture at this point.

During this mental exercise, you will find a cup and sword, which you must pick up to discover the hidden messages that they hold for you.

the second stage of your journey

1   Taking the cup or sword with you, walk farther up the mountain. Take 3–5 minutes to explore the middle reaches of the mountain. While exploring you will find the other implement. You may wish to say something as you pick it up.

2   You have now both the cup and the sword. Continue to climb to the top of the mountain. Notice the terrain and the weather, and whether there are any changes.

the third stage of your journey

1   At the top of the mountain, you will find a large flat stone on which you place the cup and the sword. Pause now and meditate for a few minutes on the cup and the sword in turn. What do each have to tell you? What insights do they offer you?

2   You might like to make a gesture involving both the cup and the sword. Make it and notice how you feel while doing it. Look at them again: have they changed in any way?

3   It is now time to go back down the mountain. You may leave one of the items at the top and return with the other. Finally, return to your safe space, your meadow.

Once you have either the cup or sword in your possession, you then need to journey farther up the mountain.

recording your experiences

Once you have taken some time to come out of your inner journey, let light into your room or put on a light. Make notes immediately to record all of your experiences. The questions below can help you remember what you experienced. Illustrate the different stages of your journey with pictures and drawings.

Illustrating the different parts of your journey is a good way of recording this exercise.

the first stage of your journey

1   How easy or difficult was it to find the path?

2   Was the path steep and rugged, or smooth and well traveled?

3   Was the weather good, or was it stormy and difficult?

4   Did the weather change when you left the meadow?

5   How easy or difficult was it to find the cup or sword?

6   What condition was the cup or sword in?

the second stage of your journey

1   Did the mountain become easier or more difficult to climb?

2   Did the weather change?

3   How easy or difficult was it to find the second item?

4   What condition was the second item in?

the third stage of your journey

1   Did the cup and the sword change
at all when you reached the top of
the mountain?

2   What did you say and do there?

3   How easy or difficult was your
descent? Had the weather changed?

4   Which did you bring back with you –
the cup or the sword – and why?

5   How does it appear to you? How do
you feel about it?

Your spiritual journey
is extremely
important, and the
energy found in the
cup (or sword) can
help you reach the
goals you have for
your everyday life.

cup

The cup is normally associated with the feminine. If you
brought the cup back with you, it suggests that you need to
relate to others at the moment. Think about how you might
spend more quality time with compatible others – friends,
family, partners. You might also want to get in touch with
your receptive and contemplative side.

sword

The sword is traditionally associated in Western culture with
the masculine. If the sword came back with you, your focus
at this time needs to be on using your dynamism and energy.
Do you have a goal or long-standing ambition that you could
use the sword's energy to help you achieve?

mountain

The mountain symbolizes your spiritual journey. Yours may
be an easy climb, or it may be a difficult one full of struggle. If
the journey is difficult, do not be daunted. When we seek
the spiritual heights, our journey can be hard, but the
rewards are great. As we climb the mountain, we reach
higher states of consciousness and new vantage points.

cup and sword

Finally, think about the appearance of the sword and the cup.
If one was tarnished or rusty, it may suggest that the relevant
part of your psyche is neglected. Has your upbringing taught
you to devalue the energy of the sword or cup or to see it
in a negative light? What can you do to give both energies
time and space in your life?

eternal
sun

In 1935, Jung was sixty. At an age when many would be retiring, he received increasing academic recognition. Academics from science, philosophy, religion, and the arts and humanities were all acknowledging the importance of Jung's work for their own disciplines. He was invited to speak at conferences and received many honors.

Jung had held no academic post at all since his resignation from the University of Zürich in 1914. Academic recognition finally came in 1935 when he was appointed Titular Professor of Psychology at the Swiss Federal Institute of Technology in Zürich. In 1936, Harvard invited him to the United States to receive an honorary degree of Doctor of Science. This was twenty-seven years after he and Freud first sailed to the U.S. to receive their honorary Doctorates of Law at Clark University. In Britain, Oxford University awarded him an honorary doctorate in 1938, and he was also elected an honorary fellow of the Royal Society of Medicine in London. In 1943, he was honored in his own country. His home city of Basel made him Professor of Medical Psychology.

In 1937, Yale invited Jung to give the prestigious Terry Lectures. Jung was an excellent speaker who could hold a large audience spellbound in either English or German, although he preferred talking

to small groups. Knowing his popularity, the Yale organizers booked a large lecture theater that would seat 3,000 with the additional promise that if numbers dwindled, the lectures would immediately move to a smaller room. The lecture series was on Psychology and Religion, and the numbers did not dwindle. The first lecture had 700 attendees. By the second lecture, word got around that this speaker was special, and the 3,000-seat hall was packed to over-flowing. Jung had a gift for communicating with people on a feeling level even if they did not understand the complexities of his theories.

After the third lecture, he joined one of the Yale professors for afternoon tea to find the professor's wife in tears. "It was your voice, your manner, the way you said things," she explained. "I felt the absolute truth of what you said. That's why I'm upset. It was beautiful." (quoted in Vincent Brome's Jung: Man and Myth).

The Final Entry by Rassouli. In the second half of his life, Jung was a popular speaker. However, he also began to withdraw regularly from society to find peace and rest.

near-death experience

The trips to India and Sri Lanka in 1938 were to be Jung's last trips outside of Europe. His travels were brought abruptly to an end by World War II. Although it was a neutral country, the war was difficult for Switzerland. Jung's son and all except one of his sons-in-law were drafted. Jung was sixty-five in 1940 and too old to join the army, so instead he worked as a volunteer doctor inside an army camp. Jung's war involvement came to a premature end in February 1944 when he succumbed to a common hazard for the elderly – he slipped in the snow and broke his ankle. Jung's doctor prescribed too much bed rest for him, and he developed an embolism. Shortly afterward, he had a heart attack. This heart attack, at the age of sixty-nine, brought him right to the brink of death.

During his "out of body" experience, Jung floated in space and looked down toward the Earth.

The real crisis actually came just after the heart attack. Like many people who are seriously ill, Jung began to feel himself detaching from his body. It was as though his consciousness was no longer imprisoned in his physical frame. He felt himself being drawn upward out of his body.

Jung found himself in space looking down upon the earth. This was before the era of space travel, so he had obviously never seen pictures of the earth from outer space. The sight was glorious. A thousand miles below, Earth was bathed in beautiful blue light. He saw seas and continents, and seemed to be floating above the southern hemisphere. He was over the island of Sri Lanka looking out northward to India, the Arabian Gulf, the Red Sea, and the Mediterranean. Significantly, these were all places that he had physically visited and which had had a profound impact on him.

Looking south, he saw an enormous block of brown granite floating in space. A similar image appeared some years later in the futuristic film 2001 – *A Space Odyssey*.

Jung came face to face with death after a heart attack at the age of sixty-nine. He had an "out of body" experience, in which he felt he was leaving his body behind.

The granite had been hewn out to make a temple. At the entrance, sitting in the lotus position, was a Hindu sage dressed in a white gown. The sage indicated that he had been expecting him. As Jung approached the temple, he felt all his past existence and experiences drop away from him like a snake's discarded skin. Only the essence of himself was left. This contained all the knowledge of what he had been and done. He simultaneously felt both great and little. There was no fear and no regret; only an acceptance of all that had been and all that was to come. Jung was about to enter a room within the temple where he sensed that he would meet all the people in his life with whom he had formed lasting connections. Suddenly, the image of his doctor appeared to him like a summons to return home. It was not yet time to leave Earth. After the near-death experience had finished, Jung's nurse told him that she had been convinced he was going to die. He seemed to be surrounded by a bright, otherworldly glow that she had only seen around someone whose life's journey had ended.

return

Like most of those who have near-death experiences, Jung returned to his body with a sense of regret. The afterlife seemed more real than life on our earthly plane. There was no choice, though, but to obey. Jung came close to death, but it was not yet his time. He still had work to do. Nevertheless, the heart attack marked a transition to old age. It was a warning that he must lead a quieter life. This was a retirement in one sense. He resigned his professorship in Zurich and spent increasing amounts of time at the retreat that he built at Bollingen. In another sense, it was a new beginning for him. The last fifteen years of Jung's life, from the age of seventy to eighty-five, were some of his most prolific years in terms of his ideas and writing.

"What is very important is to exist, and that's rarer than one realizes. To have a daily task and to accomplish it; and at the same time to attend to what is going on, inside oneself as well as outside, conscious of all life's forms, all its expressions."[1]

Toward the end of his life, Carl Jung spent more and more time at his retreat at Bollingen. The quiet surroundings gave him the peace he needed, and he wrote prolifically while staying there.

[1] From a 1959 interview with French-Swiss writer Georges Duplain in *C. G. Jung Speaking: Interviews and Encounters*, ed. William McGuire; tr. R.F. Hull (Princeton: Princeton University Press, 1977), 414.

return
to introversion

In the first half of his life, Jung established his medical career, married, and became the father of five children. To borrow an Eastern term, he fulfilled his "householder" duties to outside society. His life reached a transition point when his mother died in January 1923, at the age of seventy-five.

The death of a parent leaves us with many mixed emotions – grief, loss, release, and an awareness that there is no generation between us and mortality. Jung was forty-seven when his mother died. It was time for him to reevaluate his own life. He began to balance the extroverted demands of his outer life with an introverted need to withdraw for part of his life into silence, solitude, and the contemplation of nature. The simpler life style of the peoples he encountered in North Africa and New Mexico in the early 1920s impressed him. He was keen to emulate it and to find a way of living closer to nature. For Jung, nature meant water. He once wrote that he could not

Jung was always attracted by water and, in his later life, he built a retreat on the shores of Lake Zürich.

imagine how anyone could live without being near the presence of water. In landlocked Switzerland, water meant lakes.

It was at Bollingen, on the shores of Lake Zürich on some land that had once belonged to a monastery, that Jung decided to build himself a retreat. At first he imagined building a round one-story dwelling like an African hut, with bunks around the walls and a fire in the center. As the building work started, he decided it would be more practical to have two stories built. The structure then resembled a tower. Jung's life in Küsnacht was dominated by the needs of his family, patients, trainee analysts, and visitors seeking his wisdom. At Bollingen he found repose and renewal. Refreshed by monthly stays, he could return to Küsnacht ready to face the world.

at one with nature

Following his heart attack in 1944, the tower became for Jung a fortress in which he could retreat to write his books and think his thoughts. He was no longer able to travel the world, but the country of the mind was still open to him.

At Bollingen, he felt himself both at one with nature and at one with the human-made world. He felt part of himself in every tree. He was also within the waves washing the lake shore, the passing clouds, the falling leaves of autumn, the thrusting spring shoots, the warmth of summer sun, and the rain's fall. He felt himself part of the birds and animals that came and went in his garden. Animals loved Jung as he loved them. He was deeply attached to his dogs; he fed the birds in his garden and also fed a wild snake. Birds were so unafraid of him that one day a tit landed on his head and started to make a nest in his flowing white hair. At Bollingen, so close to nature, he developed an abiding sense of who and what we are – spiritual beings clothed in flesh, with a Self; an enduring and undying core.

At Bollingen Jung had the opportunity to become close to nature, and he enjoyed spending time in his garden with both wild and domestic animals.

brahma and atman

J ung took the term *Self* from the Hindu teaching that states "Brahman is Atman and Atman is Brahman." The Hindu word *Atman* is often translated in English as "self." In other words, he believed that at the core of our being is a divine spark, Atman, which is part of the greater whole, Brahma – that is the unknowable, infinite, and transcendent Creator of the Universe.

Many cultures have rituals that involve removing their clothing. This signifies a "letting go" of false images of themselves.

individuation

Jung's therapeutic process is more than a method of healing the sick – it is a system of spiritual transformation. The re-centering of ourselves in a new place that is not the Ego is the goal of all mystical traditions. Jung calls this process "individuation." It is a process by which we become truly individual, and truly unique. Individuation involves letting go of all the false images of ourselves that we have allowed to be built up by our environment and by the projected visions of parents, teachers, friends, and lovers. This is often symbolized in tribal initiation rites by a removal, or change of, clothing. The discovery, or recovery, of the true Self – for it is always there – is one of the aims of all of the mystical and initiatory processes.

Facing our Shadow, the inner darkness within all of us is an important part of the transformation process.

the self

Jung's message is optimistic. The psyche is purposeful, and we have a natural urge to grow to wholeness. Whatever traumas we have suffered, within us is a center that is whole and true. For those who have suffered trauma or abuse, Jung's message is one of hope. The Self is a wholeness that transcends all consciousness. It emerges from two different levels of the unconscious, the personal unconscious and the collective unconscious. As we go deeper into ourselves, we then reach the core of our personality, the bedrock, which is where the individual verges on the collective. Here we meet with the collective unconscious, or group mind of the whole of humankind. When we connect with the collective psyche, we do not lose our individuality. We become more aware of our uniqueness, at the same time recognizing that we are facets of a diamond that is the greater whole.

the process

To reach this transformation we must first let go of the Persona, our protective mask. Then we must face up to the Shadow, our own inner darkness. We must also recognize our contrasexual side, the Anima or Animus, and that this, too, is an important part of us. We must own all those aspects of ourselves that we have projected onto others. If our relationships have been based on false projections, we may find that they are no longer meaningful or right. This process can be painful for ourselves and for those close to us. Unconsciously we know all this. Part of us wants to grow and move forward. And yet part of us would be content to remain exactly where we are because it is a safe place. This is a dilemma that we must work through and resolve.

This woman has to recognize the existence of her male side, the Anima.

giving birth to the self

If we persist and go through our inner barriers, we take on a new perspective that is detached from our Egos. We unify our conscious and unconscious minds and so give birth to the Self, the hidden sun that is within us all. We become less desperate to achieve, to compete, to be bigger and better than others. Instead, we learn to value ourselves enough to give others the space to value themselves. In this way, we can enter into more genuine friendships and relationships with those around us.

ego and self

Jung observed that the Ego thinks it is master in its own house. It believes it is in control when in reality it should not be. It is important to continually remind ourselves that our Ego is only part of the mystery of our whole being.

beyond ego

The Ego is who we think we are. In part, we are right, but the Ego-ridden state is a deluded one. We think the Ego is the be all and end all of our existence; but far within us is a much deeper, wiser aspect of ourselves that has yet to be fully revealed to us. Jung's teaching indicates that the first half of our lives is for outer achievement and for satisfying the needs of the Ego. During this time we learn to support ourselves, perhaps we may become parents, and we also learn to make our contribution to the social and economic world.

The second half of life, however, has a very different purpose. It is to connect us with the deeper, wiser, and more encompassing part of ourselves that is the Self. By fulfilling our obligations to the society that has raised us, we have developed a sense of competence and self-esteem. We then begin to understand our strengths and limitations. Our Ego – our sense of "I-ness" – grows as a result. This is important, but the Ego is only the conscious part of ourselves. The Self is the whole of the psyche, both the conscious and unconscious parts. By readily accepting all of the different aspects that make up our personality, we truly become who and what we really are.

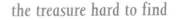

the treasure hard to find

In *Psychology and Alchemy*, Jung describes the Self as "the treasure hard to attain."[1] It lies in the ocean of the unconscious, and only the brave can reach it. In myth, self-realization is symbolized by the second stage of the hero's journey. The hero's quest leads to his coronation as King. There is Ego recognition. He acquires status. His rule is peaceful and good. Then, in many tales there is a new challenge, a spiritual quest. It may involve a descent into the Underworld to seek a treasure. In the Welsh *Mabinogion* myth cycle, King Arthur descends into the Underworld, Annwn, to retrieve the Cauldron of Rebirth. Medieval versions of the story describe Arthur's knights searching for the mystical treasure of the Holy Grail. The symbolism of the sacred quest captures the imagination still. J.R.R. Tolkien's book trilogy *The Lord of the Rings* and many modern computer games are based on this theme.

images of the self

Images of the Self appear to us both in dreams and in visions. Many of us from childhood sense an inner guiding voice that helps us through life's difficulties. This voice shows us the way forward when the conscious mind fails us. The Self can appear as a Wise Old Woman or Man. Conversely, it may also appear as a wise child or a Sun Child — ourselves reborn as perfect and unblemished beings. Often the image appears not as something human but as some sacred and holy object — the Grail, the Sun, the pearl in the lotus, the philosopher's stone, the hidden treasure.

We must learn to be in touch with all parts of our psyche. Seeing the different parts of our Self through dreams and visions helps us to accept them.

[1] C. G. Jung, *The Collected Works of Carl Jung*, vol. 12, *Psychology and Alchemy*. 2d ed. (Routledge & Kegan Paul, 1971), 518.

self and other

When first we encounter the Self, it is difficult to understand that this is truly part of ourselves. Often we project the Self onto others. We see our therapists, spiritual teachers, or worldly leaders as embodiments of the wise people we would like to be. Inevitably, they cannot live up to our projections, and disillusionment sets in.

Withdrawing from our projections and taking time to listen to the voice of the inner Divine will help us find true guidance for our lives.

withdrawing projections

When we start to dream of the Wise Old Man or the Woman who appears to us as teacher, we are beginning to withdraw from our projections and to contact the Self within. We start to listen to the inner voice of intuition and guidance, and to take responsibility for our own spiritual and personal progress. The Self is our true guru and inner guide which, in Christianity, is called the Holy Guardian Angel. It is the inner voice of wise counsel, and through it speaks the voice of the Divine.

mandalas

In Jung's inner Nekyia journey to confront the contents of his unconscious, he realized that the experiences he was undergoing paralleled those that others on the path to enlightenment in Eastern tradition had described. The journey to enlightenment was a journey to integrate the disparate parts of ourselves into a whole with a new spiritual vantage point – the Self. Often this integration can be symbolized by a mandala. At the end of World War I, when Jung's inner Nekyia journey ended, he found himself drawing mandalas. Mandala is the Sanskrit name for a circular image that is drawn, painted, danced, or enacted to assist meditation. Around the center is a symmetrical design, usually with a four-fold or eight-fold pattern. Mandalas symbolize the situation when our inner contradictions come to resolution and balance. They can also help bring the psyche to the point of balance. This is why they are widely used in spiritual work.

Within Eastern religions there are many examples of mandalas. Some Buddhist shrines are designed as complete mandalas to represent self-integration.

sanchi

There are whole temple complexes that are designed as mandalas. Jung visited one while in India, the Buddhist shrine of Sanchi. The main stupa at Sanchi is a representation of the cosmos itself. A wall surrounds it with four elaborate gates at East, South, West, and North. These are carved with animals, deities, and scenes from the life of Buddha. At each cardinal point there is a statue of the Buddha. At the center a great dome enshrines sacred relics.

Mandalas also appear in stained glass windows in Christian churches in forms such as the four Evangelists surrounding Christ at the center or four rivers flowing from the lamb. Fourfold mandala designs are found in Native American sand paintings used by shamans for healing body and mind. We also find them used in Celtic design.

Four is a number of balance; two pairs of opposites held in tension with a mediating principle at the center. A circle surrounds the pattern and holds it together. It is as though the four personality functions – thinking, feeling, sensation, and intuition – are held in balance by a fifth transcendent function that unifies them all. This transcendent function is the Self.

Ancient Celtic designs also use mandala symbols.

the voice of the self

listening to the self

For this exercise, you need quiet and privacy. You may want to light a candle and to burn some perfumed oil. You will need four large pieces of plain paper and four different-colored pens. You need to sit on the floor and lay the four pieces of paper out around you, with you in the center of them.

Gather together your paper and pens. When you are sitting in front of the candle, write the relevant headings on the tops of the pages before arranging them.

the listening exercise

1   Write a heading on each of the four pieces of paper, using different color pens. The headings are Mind, Body, Emotions, and Observer. Sit on the floor and put the Observer paper in front of you, Mind to your right, Emotions to your left, and Body behind you, to form a cross. Place the pens on top of their respective pieces of paper.

2   The Observer is wise, compassionate, and nonjudgmental. The Observer helps us get an overview of our life. To become the Observer, we must make a link to our true Self. Focus for a few minutes on the wise being that lies hidden deep within your psyche. You may find it helpful to imagine being bathed in light.

3   Now turn around to face the paper headed Body. It is important that you, rather than the papers, move. Ask yourself the following questions:
What are the strengths of my body?
What are its weaknesses?
What needs does it have that have not been met?
What steps can it take to meet that need?

4   Spend ten minutes thinking about these questions and write notes on your paper about what comes to you.

5   Turn to face your Observer paper again. Clear your psyche of the insights from your body and get in touch with your wise compassionate self.

6 Now turn to your left to the paper headed "Emotions." Ask yourself:
What are my emotional strengths?
What are my emotional weaknesses?
What emotional needs do I have that have not been met?
What steps can my emotions take to meet those needs?
Write your notes. After ten minutes or so, turn to the Observer position again and reconnect to your wise self.

7 Now do the same for "Mind." Turn to Mind paper and ask yourself:
What are the strengths of my mind?
What are its weaknesses?
What intellectual needs do I have that have not been met?
What steps can my mind take to meet those needs?
Make your notes and then return at the end to your Observer position.

8 Now turn to Body, Mind, and Emotions in turn, at your own pace and in any order. Ask each one: "Are you satisfied with our way of life? If not, is there any one thing you would like us to change so that we can cooperate creatively and incorporate this into our lifestyle?"
Record your responses.

9 Finally, turn to face the Observer place. You may have been asked to make some changes. You, the wise Observer at the center, should consider these requests carefully and realistically. Can you make them? If not, why not? If you can, when will you make them? If you cannot make the changes they request, explain why. It is important to be realistic.
For example, do not promise your body to stop smoking overnight. This is a strong addictive habit and hard to break. Promise yourself instead to make small positive changes that you know you can achieve.

10 When you have reached your decision, stay facing the Observer place and thank Body, Emotions, and Mind for their assistance and insights.

Over the next month see what you can do to use the insights you have gained to make positive changes in your life. This is an exercise to help you realize that you are not just your body, emotions, or mind, but that there is a deeper, wiser person within you that is your true Self. The Self is a source of loving wisdom and wise insight. Try and take a few moments each day to be still and to listen to the wise person within.

journey's goal

Switzerland saw the elderly Carl Jung as one of her leading citizens. Famous for its mountains and financial banks, Switzerland had few nationals so well-known on the world's stage. In 1946, when Winston Churchill visited Switzerland, it was Carl Jung who was seated beside him at a gala dinner. His opinion was widely sought by the Swiss press, professional bodies, and the authorities.

Politically, Jung favored strong ties between Europe and the United States. He saw it as America's role to lead the West in its stand against totalitarian systems. He was strongly opposed to communism. He saw it as a system that would quash human individuality and growth. He also feared the dangers of the nuclear arms race and nuclear proliferation.

Many people saw Jung as a "Mana-personality," a kind of contemporary shaman with special powers. The Jungian analyst, Dr. Arwind Vasavada, records that when he made his first visit to Jung, he could not prevent himself from treating Jung as he would a distinguished Indian guru. He prostrated himself at his feet. Tactfully, Jung helped him up.

Jung is widely credited as being a major influence in the founding of Alcoholics Anonymous (AA), and Bill Wilson, its co-founder, paid many tributes to him. Jung recognized that the alcoholics' craving for alcohol was an equivalent thirst to the more powerful, deeper spiritual thirst each one of us has.

People sought Jung's opinion on everything from life after death to the existence of God. The scientist in Jung did not always welcome such questions. In a conversation with a Jesuit priest, he once exclaimed, "It is quite clear that God exists, but why are people always asking me to prove this psychologically?" (from Father Raymond Hostie's *Religion and the Psychology of Jung*). Like Buddha, he believed it was foolish to engage in pointless intellectual speculation about things that were unprovable. We do not learn about the Divine through our thinking function. Jung believed that our understanding of the Divine came through spiritual experience mediated by feeling, intuition, and, perhaps, sensation.

In his old age, Jung seemed to be like a medieval magus or a Chinese sage, the archetype of the Wise Old Man. He had always had an extraordinarily strong presence that conveyed an air of spiritual greatness and total well-being. People also remembered his fun and laughter – his wisdom was balanced by mirth.

Two Infinities by Rassouli. In the last years of his life, Jung was an important figure in society. On a more personal level, he had recognized the need to find the inner Divine and was content with his own life.

red king, white queen

The two important women who shared most of Jung's life were fated to die before him. Toni Wolff died in 1953. Although she had been troubled by severe arthritis, her death was a sudden and unexpected one. Emma died two years after.

Toni and Emma, the dual carriers of Jung's Anima, provided him with very different things. Emma was the queen who sanctified his home; Toni the guide to his creative work.

After Toni's death, Jung took up stone-carving to balance the emotional demands of therapy and the intellectual demands of his writing. At Bollingen he planned a stone in memory of Toni with a Chinese symbol on it meaning "She was the fragrance of the house."

Jung in 1953, the year his long-term helpmate, Toni Wolff, died. Jung was seventy-eight.

In November 1955, Emma Jung also died — of cancer. She had deteriorated rapidly, but fortunately, her death was peaceful and painless. Emma's loss was a terrible blow to Jung. Their marriage had lasted fifty-three years. Emma was greatly loved by her family, patients, and by those who trained as Jungian analysts. Jung wrote that in a marriage one person "contains" the other. He had thought that he contained Emma, but, in reality, it was she who provided the stable framework that enabled him to do his life's work. She played the traditional role of wife selflessly and with great love, and was the mother of the family that, particularly in later years, came to mean so much to him. By the time of his death, Jung had nineteen grandchildren and ten great-grandchildren. Together with his five children and their spouses, this made up an enormous and very supportive family group for Jung. Throughout her life, Emma had provided him with security, stability, and a base in which his ideas could brew and transform like the elixir in the alchemist's spherical vessel, and now his family was to support him emotionally in his last years.

> "She was a queen! She was a queen!"

> "She was the foundation of my house"

Emma had been Jung's solidity, giving him the support and freedom he needed for his life's work.

bereavement

At Emma's funeral, the church was filled to overflowing. Afterward, Jung was found in his study weeping. Over and over again, he said, "She was a queen! She was a queen!" At Bollingen, Jung carved another stone, this time in memory of Emma. On it was a Chinese symbol meaning "She was the foundation of my house."

For the first few months after her death, Jung had no sense of contact with Emma. He wrote to his daughter Marianne, "Mamma's death has left a gap for me that cannot be filled."[1]

There was only emptiness and silence. Then he had a dream. He entered an empty and darkened theater, but with a brilliantly lit stage. Between the audience and the stage was a deep orchestra pit that he could not cross. His wife was on stage, more beautiful than ever he had seen her. Later, he had another dream. They were together in Provence, in the south of France, pursuing the Grail studies that Emma had been working on before her death. Jung sensed with relief that beyond the grave Emma was still traveling forward on her spiritual journey.

Jung with his wife and family in 1918. His family had always meant a great deal to him, but after his wife's death in 1955 he came to rely on his children for emotional support.

[1] Letter of July 17, 1956 in C. G. Jung, *Letters, Vol. 11: 1951–1961*, ed. G. Alder; tr. R. F. C. Hull (Princeton: Princeton University Press, 1953).

the evening of jung's life

Jung's four daughters and his daughter-in-law took turns to come and stay with him for short periods, but he could not manage alone. In this dark time of his life, Jung was helped by the intrepid ex-nurse, Ruth Bailey, who had trekked with him through East Africa some thirty years before. Ruth Bailey had become a lifelong friend of Carl and Emma, spending vacations with them every year. "Come and see me out," he asked her. "You are good at seeing people out."[1] Now elderly herself, she uprooted herself from England and came to Switzerland to be his housekeeper.

Carl and Ruth divided their time between Küsnacht and Bollingen. At Bollingen, they lived a simple lifestyle without gas or electricity. Chores were shared. Jung chose the menus, Ruth Bailey prepared the food, and Jung cooked it. In the evenings they sat looking out over the lake and reading.

After all the demands of the earlier years, Jung took great delight in living a peaceful and contemplative life. He appreciated Ruth Bailey's common sense and calm temperament. He also thought she had learned a most wonderful gift — the gift of silence. His own death held no fear for him. He had sensed others in the after-life, and certain personal experiences had inclined him to believe in the Hindu and Buddhist idea that we could live more than once. He had a strong attraction to England. In later life he could easily have been mistaken for an Englishman. One explanation he considered was that he had lived there in a former life. In midlife, Jung wrote that few people are artists in life and that the art of living life to the full was the most difficult art of all. Jung's own afternoon of life had been as fruitful as the morning, and in its evening, Jung wrote that he was satisfied with the course his life had taken. Some aspects of his life had been unhappy, but even these darker times were woven into a tapestry that made a complete and fulfilled whole. Now evening was drawing to a close.

> "A sense of a wider meaning to one's existence is what raises a man beyond merely getting and spending. If he lacks this sense, he is lost and miserable."[2]

[1] Vincent. Brome, *Jung: Man and Myth* (Granada, 1980), 262.
[2] Carl G. Jung, and Marie-Louise von Franz, eds., *Man and His Symbols* (Aldus, 1964), 89.

From the "Bern" Series by Robert Natkin. The sun was setting on Jung's life and, just before he died, he asked to see the beautiful sunset outside his window for one last time.

Jung kept working on some final writings on symbolism until just before his death. He died at his home in Küsnacht, Zürich, at the age of eighty-five. During his last three days, it seemed to Ruth Bailey that he was in some far-off country where he saw wonderful and beautiful things. He began to dream that the "other Bollingen," a spiritual parallel of his tower, was complete and ready for habitation.

At the beginning of his midlife crisis, Jung dreamed of a beautiful sunrise above a mountain and of the death of Siegfried, his Ego image. Now it was sunset and time for another death. On the last evening of his life, his son Franz was with him and also Ruth Bailey. As Ruth left the room, he asked Franz to quickly help him out of bed before she came back

and stopped him. He wanted to look at the sunset. The summer sun sank like a ball of red flame beneath the Alps. Their peaks, painted first in gold and then pink, orange, and rose, faded to blue-black shadow and darkness. Jung returned to his bed for the last time.

Jung died on June 6, 1961. A little while before his death, he had a dream where he was high on a mountain looking at a boulder bathed in sunlight. Carved in the stone were the words:

"Take this as a sign of the wholeness you have achieved, and the singleness you have become."

His physical progeny live after him; so too do his books, ideas, vision – and, perhaps, part of himself. Many have felt that Jung's presence still lingers at the lakeside tower at Bollingen.

death and the afterlife

Jung always called death "the Great Adventure." He believed that what came after death was "unspeakably glorious." Between each life were wondrous experiences that gave insight into totally different modes of existence. Like Hindus and Buddhists, he believed we might inherit karma in the form of particular personality characteristics, susceptibility to certain diseases, and special gifts.

taoism

Other ideas developed from Jung's encounters with Chinese Taoist thought. This was a major influence on Jung's understanding of linear time.

Jung's understanding of Taoism began to develop when in 1922, he met Richard Wilhelm, a famous expert on Chinese culture. Originally, Richard Wilhelm went to China as a missionary, but Christianity was of little interest to the Chinese. Wilhelm instead found himself studying the Chinese language, as well as their philosophy, religion, and culture. An immediate rapport developed between the two men. Their eight-year relationship was as significant for Jung as his relationship with Freud, but here there was no tension between a surrogate son and father. Jung and Wilhelm met as equals. The relationship ended only with Wilhelm's untimely death, which saddened Jung greatly.

Jung found Richard Wilhelm an important friend with whom he could discuss Chinese culture and religion.

A divination can be performed by throwing yarrow stalks. Jung had already tried this before meeting Wilhelm, but when they became friends, Wilhelm encouraged him to experiment further.

the secret of the golden flower

In much of Jung's work, we find the theme of the balancing of opposites within. He states that thinking must be balanced with feeling, sensation with intuition, extroversion with introversion, feminine with masculine, and materialism with spirituality. Many of Jung's ideas about integration of opposites were derived from Eastern traditions. When he came to provide a commentary for Richard Wilhelm's translation of *The Secret of the Golden Flower*, Jung discovered the image of the journey around the center, the circumambulation, which led to the integration of the opposites and contradictions within. This Chinese text seemed to Jung to contain in symbolic form all the insights he had gained about the human psyche from his own work with patients. The ancient sages had explored the same territory.

[1] Quoted in C. G. Jung's Commentary on "The Secret of the Golden Flower" (1929) in *The Collected Works of C. G. Jung*, vol. 13, *Alchemical Studies*, 2d ed. (Routledge & Kegan Paul, 1971), para. 64.

> "*A halo of light surrounds the world of the law.*
>
> *We forget one another, quiet and pure, all-powerful and empty.*
>
> *The emptiness is irradiated by the light of the heart of heaven.*
>
> *The water of the sea is smooth and mirrors the moon in its surface.*
>
> *The clouds disappear in blue space; the mountains shine clear.*
>
> *Consciousness reverts to contemplation; the moon-disk rests alone.*"[1]

The I-Ching Chinese coin, which contains images of Chinese zodiacal figures.

synchronicity

Before he met Richard Wilhelm, Jung had already tried experimenting with the Chinese yarrow-stalk divination system, the "I Ching." Richard Wilhelm helped Jung develop his famous idea of synchronicity, or meaningful coincidence, that he used to explain divination. Divination systems such as the I Ching, tarot, and astrology can provide instantaneous "snapshots" of where we are and the patterns of energy that surround us. Events in the future can be read from the patterns of the present. Jung's study of divination led him to believe that our everyday understanding of the nature of time and space was limited. Jung's ideas about synchronicity also evolved from meetings with famous quantum physicists, such as Albert Einstein, Wolfgang Pauli, and Werner Heisenberg. Time does not go forward in a straight line. Time, space, and events coexist in a way that is beyond the normal understanding of our ordinary senses. However, the concept is understood by leading scientists today as it was by the ancient mysticisms and esoteric teachings of East and West.

the "i ching"

The "I Ching" or "Book of Changes" is a divination system based on ancient Chinese Taoist thought. A divination is performed by casting traditional yarrow stalks or more simply Chinese coins. These can fall into one of sixty-four possible patterns or hexagrams. The hexagrams have interpretations given by the revered sage Confucius and his followers, and these provide guidance about how best to act in a given situation.

Tarot cards are one type of divination that can hold clues about the past and the future.

beyond death

If time is illusory, and space and events coexist, the nature of existence is very different from what our senses tell us. Beyond the physical body may lie a realm of consciousness that is completely different from what we experience when alive. Jung was aware that the concepts of synchronicity and quantum physics had implications for life after death.

life's afternoon

Jung's paranormal experiences had shown him that the psyche was not confined in space and time. His out-of-body experience in 1944 had done much to conquer his fear of death. He once wrote to a Catholic priest that he knew that consciousness was not confined to the body. Jung believed that we should be aware of the inevitability of death and that, at the same time, we should live life to the fullest for the whole of our life. Western society often treats middle and old age as disastrous stages of decline that have no purpose. Jung believed that the second half of life was as important as the first. In the ancient world, the pagan mystery schools taught

In later years we need goals and hobbies to satisfy our thirst for personal growth.

a vision for living

By accepting that we will all eventually die, we can move on to enjoy our lives, at whatever age we are.

Jung believed that five things are necessary for human happiness in the second half of life. First, we need good physical and mental health. Second, we need good personal and intimate relationships, such as those of marriage, family, and friends. We also need to be able to see the beauty of the world. The capacity for perceiving beauty in art and nature is the third dimension necessary for human happiness. Fourth, we need a reasonable standard of living and satisfactory work. Last, but not least, we need a philosophical or spiritual point of view that can help us cope with life's difficulties and provide us with an ethical basis on which to live our lives.

Jung believed that the East understood much more about the spiritual dimension of the second part of life than the West did.

the message of the second half of life. In tribal society, there were rites by which people became respected elders. Jung believed that if there was no purpose to the second half of life, nature would not have increased our lifespan beyond our reproductive days. Mere moneymaking would not satisfy us in the second half of life. In midlife onward, we need what Jung called "culture" – the personal growth that can come through the arts, therapy, spirituality, and religion. We need ongoing goals for which we can strive. Jung's own life was an epitome of this.

inner journey

Jung believed that the East understood much better than the West the purpose of the second half of life. In the East, it is common to abandon worldly pursuits in midlife and to devote oneself to the spiritual life. Westerners pursue the spiritual life by seeking God outside of ourselves. In Eastern tradition, God is within, and we can attain union with the Divine through sincere spiritual practice and dedication. For Jung, the second half of life is for discovering the Divine within.

achieving balance

What Jung advocates is balance. If we have concentrated in the first half of life on worldly achievement, then to redress the balance in the second half of life, we will need to focus on our relationships. Relationships with partners, children, grandchildren, and friends become important sources of satisfaction.

Relationships

Other satisfactions come from an active spiritual life and from stimulating the mind. For those who have concentrated on the job of parenting and relationships, in the second half of life other aspects will need to be developed. Women, for instance, who have been devoted to motherhood and the needs of others, may find that intellectual stimulation and spiritual quest become important to balance the psyche.

a modern spirituality

For Jung, the primary task of the second half of life is to work toward life's ultimate goal – individuation and a realization of the Self within. For this we need a spiritual perspective. This can be found in one of the world religions or on a more individual path. Jung is openminded in his approach and does not make value judgments about which variety of spirituality was best or most true. He prided himself on the fact that after his analysis, Jews become better Jews, Catholics better Catholics. In other words, we become better equipped to follow our own spiritual quest. It is the journey, not the baggage we take with us, that is important. The forms our different paths to the Divine take should not be the focus of our thoughts. They are but the ever-changing blossoms and leaves of the tree of all eternal wisdom.

Our relationships with our grandchildren can be particularly rewarding for both us and them.

Jung believed that we can find the Divine within each of us and that Christ is a symbol of inner unity.

a social purpose

Many political creeds have endeavored to create a Utopia for their own country – the perfect society. However, they all try to do so by changing the basic structure of their society. However, they must realize that society is the creation of those who live in it. If the society is deficient, it is because we are ourselves are deficient. In order to create social harmony, we must first find harmony within ourselves; otherwise, our vision of what constitutes social harmony will be false and distorted by the flaws within each of our own personalities. By freeing ourselves from the barriers that prevent us from developing our abilities fully, we are then better able to use those abilities constructively for others and for the society at large. We are also better able to relate to others. This is important for ourselves as individuals, as well as important for each of our societies. The evolution of individuals is essential if society as a whole is to survive.

the mysteries

The spiritual quest for God is in part an inner psychological journey. Jung believed that spiritual teachers such as Christ and Buddha are both historical beings and symbols of the inner unity that we are all striving to attain throughout our lifetimes. "Christ is within" is what Jung's teaching is saying to us. This is not to denigrate the spiritual quest or, by a process of reductionism, to turn it into mere psychology. Jung, through his own spiritual journey, came to recognize that "if that which thou seekest thou findest not within thee, thou wilt never find it without thee."[1] Jungian analysts today still strongly believe that the Divine is present within us, as well as in the world outside and beyond.

[1] From the "Great Mother Charge" quoted in Crowley, V. *Wicca: The Old Religion in the New Millennium*. (Thorsons/HarperCollins, 1996), p 191.

going forward
on our journey

We can feel we are being selfish or even self-indulgent if we seek psychological and spiritual transformation when life is so busy and demanding. It can be hard to set aside time for ourselves, but Jung believed that inner transformation is an important task and responsibility, not just for our own spiritual attainment, but also for our communities at large.

analysis

To begin to explore the unconscious using Jung's methods, the best starting point is to attend lectures, workshops, or other events where you can hear Jung's ideas discussed and do some preliminary experiential work. Another option is to undertake Jungian therapy with an analyst trained by a recognized organization. As analysis is a process which may last for several years, it should not be undertaken lightly. For those unable to afford the full fees, some institutes are able to offer reduced fees with analysts in training. Each individual case is truly individual.

workshops

Workshops on themes related to Jungian psychology take place in many major cities. You can find events listed at the Jung institutes referred to at the end of this book. Bookstores with large psychology and spirituality sections often carry leaflets advertising local events as well as magazines with events listings. Many workshops use particular creative approaches to explore Jung's work, for instance, art, dream analysis, writing, poetry, and storytelling. In addition to

Jung's work still has an important place in the world today. There are many ways to discover more about his teachings. Try something practical like a workshop, lecture, or even Jungian analysis for yourself.

providing referral services, many Jungian institutes have programs of lectures and workshops that are open to the public, and publish books and journals on Jung's work. You can also find events listings through Jungian institutes on the Web sites right. Many religious groups are interested in Jung's work. The Christian retreat movement runs workshops on Jungian-related themes. Information can be found in Christian bookstores and Catholic religious outlets.

further reading

Most bookstores have books by and about Jung. A good starting point is to read his autobiography, *Memories, Dreams, Reflections*, recorded and edited by Aniela Jaffé and translated by R. and C. Winston, London: Fontana Paperback, 1995.

As an introduction to his complex work, try reading Carl G. Jung and Marie-Louise von Franz, eds., *Man and His Symbols*. London: Aldus, 1964. There are also later paperback editions. This book, written toward the end of Jung's life, was his first book addressed to the general reader rather than to academic specialists.

Carl G. Jung, *The Portable Jung*, edited by Joseph Campbell, New York: Penguin, 1976, is a useful book of extracts from Jung's writings.

Vivianne Crowley, *Principles of Jungian Spirituality*, London: Thorsons/HarperCollins, 1998, is an introduction to Jung's work on spirituality.

Try researching some of Jung's own material, as well as reading some of the countless books written about him and his work.

web sites

There is a vast amount of information about Carl Jung, his works, and Jungian organizations on the Worldwide Web. These addresses are good starting points:

http://www.cgjung.com and

http://www.iaap.org

Both have links to other Jungian sites. You could also do a search on "Carl Jung" or "C. G. Jung."

groups and organizations

Institutes and organizations dedicated to teaching and developing Jung's work exist throughout the world and the list below is only a small selection of them. When considering analysis, you are advised to contact a practitioner through an institute that can verify his or her credentials. There are Jungian groups and institutes in non-English speaking countries as well, most notably the C. G. Jung Institute of Analytical Psychology in Kilchberg (near Zürich), Switzerland.

Aradia Trust, BM DEOSIL
London WC1N 3XX, UK.
(Runs Vivianne and Chris Crowley's British workshops on Psychology of the Sacred and on personality type).

Association of Jungian Analysts
7 Eton Avenue,
London NW3 3EL, UK.

Australian and New Zealand Society of Jungian Analysts (ANZSJA)
34 Swanson Way, Ocean Reef,
Perth WA 6027, Australia.

British Association of Psychotherapists (the Jungian section)
37 Mapesbury Road, London NW2 4HJ, UK.

C.G. Jung Analysts of the Greater Washington, D.C. Metropolitan Area
5725 MacArthur Blvd. N.W.,
Washington, D.C., 20016, USA.

C.G. Jung Institute of Chicago
1567 Maple Avenue, Evanston,
Illinois 60201, USA.

C.G. Jung Institute of Los Angeles
10349 West Pico Blvd., Los Angeles,
California 90064, USA.

C.G. Jung Society of New Mexico
908 Old Santa Fe Trail, Santa Fe, New Mexico 87501-4557, USA.

C.G. Jung Institute Pacific Northwest
Dr. James S Witzig, 3690 Knob Hill Lane, Eugene, Oregon 97405, USA.

C.G. Jung Institute of San Francisco
2040 Gough St., San Francisco, CA 94109, USA.

Centre for Transpersonal Psychology
86a Marylebone High Street, London W1M 3DE, UK.
(The center runs excellent workshops and training courses on Jungian themes throughout Britain and in Ireland.)

**Dallas Society of
Jungian Analysts**

PO Box 7004, Dallas, Texas 75209-
0004, USA.

Guild of Pastoral Psychology

PO Box 1107,

London W3 6ZP, UK.

(This is not a training institute but a forum
for people interested in Jungian psychology
and religion. It has lectures, seminars,
and conferences.)

**International Group of
Analytical Psychologists**

PO Box 1175,

London W3 6DS, UK.

**Inter-Regional Society of
Jungian Analysts**

4135 Brownsville Road, Pittsburgh,

Pennsylvania 15227, USA.

Jungian Analysts – North Pacific

2010 Waverly Place North No. 1,

Seattle, Washington 98109, USA.

**New England Society of
Jungian Analysts (NESJA)**

C.G. Jung Institute-Boston,

116 St. Botolph Street, Boston,

Massachusetts 02115, USA.

**New York Association for
Analytical Psychology**

28 East 39th Street, New York,

NY 10016, USA.

**Ontario Association of
Jungian Analysts**

223 St Clair Avenue West, Toronto,

Ontario M4V 1R3, Canada.

**Philadelphia Association of
Jungian Analysts**

119 Coulter Avenue, Ardmore,

Pennsylvania 19003-2427, USA.

Society of Analytical Psychology

1 Daleham Gardens,

London NW3 5BY, UK.

**South African Association of
Jungian Analysts**

4 Linray Road, Rosebank,

7700 Capetown, South Africa.

index